THE GLORIES
OF THE
PRECIOUS BLOOD

GW00671591

THE GLORIES
OF THE
PRECIOUS BLOOD

By

REV. MAX F. WALZ C. PP. S.

"Who is this that cometh from Edom with dyed garments from Bosra? This beautiful one in his robe, walking in the greatness of his strength. I, that speak justice, and am a defender to save.

Why then is thy apparel red, and thy garments like theirs that tread in the winepress?"
—Isaias 63:1

TAN BOOKS AND PUBLISHERS, INC.
Rockford, Illinois 61105

Imprimi Potest: Joseph M. Marling, C.PP.S., Ph.D.
Provincial C.PP.S.

Nihil Obstat: J. E. Dillon, Censor

Imprimatur: John Francis Noll, D.D.
Bishop of Ft. Wayne

Feast of the Ascension
May 18, 1939

ISBN: 978-0-89555-889-3

Printed and bound in the United States of America.

TAN BOOKS AND PUBLISHERS, INC.
P.O. Box 424
Rockford, Illinois 61105
2008

To the
Immaculate Heart of Mary
the fountain-head
of the
Blood of our Redeemer
this little volume
is affectionately dedicated
by the author
with the prayer
that our Blessed Lady
by her powerful intercession
may draw for us all
much love and many graces
from the fountains of the Precious Blood
in the
Chalice of Benediction

Contents

PART I

Foreword ix

Foreword to Second Edition xiii

CHAPTER   PAGE

1. The Vision 3

2. The Foreshadowing 10

3. The Rosy Dawn 14

4. This Beautiful One in His Robe 20

5. Why Is Thy Apparel Red? 29

6. My Blood Is Drink Indeed 39

7. With Dyed Garments 45

8. Plentiful Redemption 53

9. Reparation 59

10. The Blood Shall Be Unto You for a Sign 66

11. Balm for the Sick and Consolation
    for the Dying 72

12. Redemption for the Souls in Purgatory 79

13. A Voice in the Concert of the Elect 86

Devotion to the Precious Blood
PART II

1. Its Nature and Practice 95

2. A Devotion for Every Christian 110

3. The Devotion of the Elect 115

4. Growth and Development 120

5. An Apostle of the Precious Blood 125

Foreword

BLOOD was the first appeal of earth to Heaven. "The voice of thy brother's blood crieth to me from the earth." (*Gen.* 4:10). But the voice of the Blood of Jesus, "the Lamb which was slain from the beginning of the world." (*Apoc.* 13:8) and which is daily on our altars "as if immolated" (*Apoc.* 5:6), cries without intermission to Heaven—not for vengeance, as did the blood of Abel, but for pardon, grace and mercy for us all.

Devotion to the Precious Blood, which is therefore as old as the world, affords us a better understanding of the worship of the Old Law, in which blood was a characteristic feature, while it leads us into the very heart of our holy religion by explaining the sacrificial Blood of the New Testament, and by bringing home to our minds and hearts its power and efficacy in the Mass and in the Sacraments.

It is a devotion of the "Mystery of Faith," of the inexpressible love of Jesus in pouring out His Blood for us on the Cross and shedding it mystically on thousands of altars as the price of our redemption and the heavenly drink of our souls.

This devotion fills us with a warmth of love not suspected by those who are unacquainted with its nature and practice. In the Mass the Church prays that the offering of the "chalice of salvation" may ascend in the sight of the divine Majesty "with the odor of sweetness."

St. Paul says: "Christ hath loved us, and hath delivered Himself for us, an oblation, and a sacrifice to God for an odor of sweetness." (*Eph.* 5:2).

If, therefore, the offering of the Eucharistic Blood of Jesus is "an odor of sweetness" to God, the practical part of the devotion to the Precious Blood, which consists in the oblation of this divine Blood, must be most pleasing and acceptable to the Triune God.

In the offering to God of the sacrificial Blood of the altar, as an oblation of homage and propitiation as well as an act of atonement for their own sins and those of others, the faithful will find at all times a copious outlet for their devotion to the Precious Blood.

Those who are oppressed by the memory of their sins, diffident about the efficacy of their prayers or doubtful about their salvation, should experience an awakening of confidence in the devotion to the Blood of the Atonement. "Having therefore, brethren, a confidence in the entering into the holies by the blood of Christ." (*Heb.* 10:19).

The Blood of Jesus has been fittingly called "Precious Blood" by the Prince of the Apostles, because:

1. The bloody rites, as a figure of our unbloody sacrifice, were an essential part of the accepted religion of the Old Law, and because the foreseeing of the shedding of the Divine Blood caused God to flood the world with mercies.

2. It had its source in the Immaculate Heart of Mary.

3. It is the Divine Blood which throughout eternity flows in and out of the Heart of Jesus.

4. It is the Price of our Redemption, because it reconciled us to God, and opened to mankind the sealed gates of Heaven.

5. It is the power, the voice, of the Sacred Heart ever pleading for us in the Mass.

6. It is this Blood that procures super-abundant life

for us in the Sacraments, and is thereby a means of Protection, Intercession, Expiation and Sanctification.

7. It is the burden of the Song of the Elect. "Thou art worthy, O Lord . . . because thou wast slain, and hast redeemed us to God, in thy blood, out of every tribe, and tongue, and people, and nation, and hast made us to our God a kingdom." (*Apoc.* 5:9, 10).

Foreword to the
Second and Revised Edition

THIS book was first published in 1914. Since then it has been out of print for a number of years. Immediately after the first appearance, it was translated into French with the permission of the author.

Cardinal Bégin, Archbishop of Quebec, graciously wrote a beautiful introduction to the French edition.

Recently the author was agreeably surprised to learn that the book was transcribed and set also in Braille for the benefit of the blind.

This same book is now published [1939] with the original title but under a different arrangement and new reading matter.

The writer of these pages has attempted to portray Our Lord and Redeemer as the Prophet Isaias has visioned Him centuries before when he says: "Who is this that cometh from Edom, with dyed garments from Bosra?" whom he calls "this beautiful one in his robe." He then elicits our further and deepest interest by asking "why then is thy apparel red, and thy garments like theirs that tread in the winepress?"

PART I

Chapter 1

The Vision

Who is this that cometh from Edom, with dyed garments from Bosra? This beautiful one in his robe, walking in the greatness of his strength. I, that speak justice, and am a defender to save.

Why then is thy apparel red, and thy garments like theirs that tread in the winepress?

—Isaias 63:1-2

THE Evangelist unfolds the picture which the Prophet Isaias had in mind and at the same time verifies his prophecy when he tells us that He "came forth."

Who is that that came forth? The King of kings and the Lord of lords, who looks upon the earth and causes it to tremble; the fountain of sanctity, before whom the angels are not pure; the sun of eternal splendor, who dwelleth in light inaccessible; the Desire of the eternal hills; the Expected of the Nations, for whom all Israel sighed for over four thousand years.

Where does He come forth? In the city of Jerusalem, the capital of Judea, and at a time when the chosen people of God were gathered together from all parts of the world to celebrate their greatest feast. He came forth before the high council and chiefs of the whole Jewish race. He came forth before the representative of the great Roman Empire.

3

How did He come forth in this wonderful and dramatic setting? The long awaited Messias did not come forth in the gorgeous habiliments of an oriental potentate. He did not come forth like Moses from the mountain in dazzling light, striking terror into the hearts of the people. He did not come forth in the fiery chariot of an Elias. "Jesus came forth," writes the beloved disciple, "bearing the crown of thorns, and the purple garment." He came forth His body mangled and covered with Blood from head to foot. This is the vision the Prophet had when he exclaims: Who is this that cometh with dyed garments, and he expressly calls Him beautiful, just as He is beautiful in this royal robe of His own Precious Blood to all the lovers and followers of the Crucified.

Why then is thy apparel red? Because red is the color of blood, and because it speaks of royalty and divine love. Purple denotes beauty, splendor, preciousness. "My beloved is white and ruddy." (*Cant.* 5:10). His entire body is crimsoned with His own Blood because in the language of the disciple whom Jesus loved, "God *so* loved the world." Because He wanted to set His inexpressible love in everlasting rubrics. Because Jesus was pouring out His Heart's Blood to prove that no man hath greater love than he who lays down his life for his friends. Because He loved me and delivered Himself up for me, as St. Paul reminds us. In this apparel, then, He came forth and although trembling with pain, He is walking through the streets of Jerusalem to Mount Calvary "in the greatness of His strength"—which is His love.

Once during the public life of Our Lord when the good people wanted to make Him their king, He fled. But now that He is wearing the Crown of Thorns beset with the ruby gems of His Divine Blood and wearing the purple mantle, which has taken on the hue of the "dyed garments from Bosra," by contact with His bleeding body, He proclaims Himself King.

It is in this prophetic livery that Pilate unconsciously wants us to see the vision of Isaias when he presents Jesus to the people with the words, "behold the man," "behold your king." These words coming down the centuries should re-echo in our souls until our sinful passions are hushed; until the bite of the fiery serpent is healed; until our hearts are all aflame with love for "this beautiful one in His robe." During His Passion, Our Divine Saviour is silent. But the Blood dripping from many wounds gives a heartrending utterance to His speechless love.

No feast day can so grip the hearts of the faithful and cause the hot tears of love and compunction to well up in their eyes as does Good Friday, when Our Blessed Redeemer appears in the vision of Isaias, in the vesture of His Blood, which manifests Him in the greatest ardor of His incomprehensibly and ineffably tender and compassionate love, and when the faithful in a loving embrace imprint a kiss upon the feet of the Divine Victim—the only communion permitted on that day.

They who cannot envision Jesus eye to eye with the inspired writers and do not feel drawn rather than repelled by the bloody sight of their Saviour in His Passion cannot claim that they are faithful followers of Christ. They are woefully ignorant of the divine unction that flows from the Redeemer's bleeding wounds. "But now in Christ Jesus, you, who sometime were afar off, are made nigh by the blood of Christ." (*Eph.* 2:13).

To see blood flow from a human body excites in us revulsive feelings, but the sight moves us likewise to sympathy and compassion. The blood of our corrupt nature has the taint and smell of sin, but the Blood of Christ coming from the most pure source, the Immaculate Heart of the Virgin Mary, and by its hypostatic union with the Godhead being divine, has an odor of sweetness, and while it does remind us in the Passion that a life is ebbing out, it assures that this redeeming Blood is in fact imparting to us a more abundant life—a divine life by transfusion in the Sacraments.

The first part of this book sets forth Our Divine Redeemer in the red apparel of His own Blood. "Red is the color of the most glaring light—of fire." "I am come to cast fire on the earth: and what will I but that it be kindled?" (*Luke* 12:49). All aflame with the wounds of His Love He enters the combat. This is the way the Seer of Patmos sees Him in the triumph of His love. "He was clothed with a garment sprinkled with blood." (*Apoc.* 19:13).

The fiery furnace in which the three young men sang their canticle of praise was heated seven times more than ordinarily. But the divine furnace of Christ's Sacred Heart was heated infinitely more by the fire of His love when Jesus poured out His Blood seven times for us. The flames from this "fiery furnace" are ever issuing forth setting millions of hearts on fire to sing their canticle of praise to "Jesus Who with His Blood hath saved us."

After this divine love-flame has set our hearts on fire with this sacrificial love, we will no longer shrink from the mangled body of Our Saviour in His Passion, but will find in it a most prolific source of divine comfort and strength.

Blood of Christ, inebriate me. Make me drunk with Thy love, with the unutterable love of Thy Sacred Heart. Blood of Christ, inebriate me with the love of Thy Sorrowful Mother, with the love of Thy martyrs and saints.

The world is drunk with power; intoxicated with its own conceit; maddened with the urge to quaff from the muddy streams of mundane pleasures.

Blood of Christ, be a tonic to my soul, that it may become strong to turn away from the flesh pots of Egypt and the cup of Babylon and thirst after the torrents of Thy delights, so that it may realize that without suffering there is no love and that without love there is no zeal.

Hence our devotion must turn to a practical purpose. Just as the Consecration forms the center and summit of the Mass, so a particular devotion to the world-redeeming Blood finds its highest expression in the same Eucharistic Sacrifice. The practical part of this age-old devotion consists in the oblation of the Precious Blood.

When the chalice has been raised on high at the elevation, the faithful should offer to the Heavenly Father the Precious Blood of His well-beloved Son to render Him propitious to their petitions. In this manner they will interpose the Blood of the New Testament between themselves and God, who will look with supreme complacency upon their supplications on account of the Blood of the Atonement which speaks better than the blood of Abel which cried to Heaven for vengeance.

St. Paul speaks of the "voice" of the Precious Blood which will plead for us at the throne of God, and this voice will plead with trumpet tones in the Holy Sacrifice of the Mass and with the same efficacy ("clamore valido") as it did when it dripped from the Sacred Wounds of the Crucified.

When you thus offer the "Chalice of Salvation" for yourselves or others, for the sick and dying, for the conversion of sinners, or for the Poor Souls in Purgatory, you are not praying alone, but the Blood that appeased the wrath of the Father on account of our sinful race, the Blood that opened Heaven for you and obtained all the graces you need to reach it, will plead with you and for you with all the appeal of the bleeding and agonizing Heart of Jesus.

The suffering souls in Purgatory will be most grateful for the offerings of the Precious Blood in their behalf. They long for it more than the parched earth does for a refreshing rain. You are actually paying the price for their redemption. In doing so you will be getting a thrill out of the Mass which perhaps you never experienced before. All this is, of course, in harmony with the Liturgical Movement, because you are offering with the priest, and it can be done in a few moments of time.

Christ stands before us today as He did in the vision of Isaias, as He stood in the tribunal of Pilate, in the red apparel of His love, challenging us to Catholic Action; to choose between Him and Barabbas; to follow the crimsoned standard of the Cross, or the red flag of Communism.

"We have a God to love and the King of kings to fight for. The whole mentality of the world is in opposition to the Kingdom of Christ." But that pitiful figure dripping with Blood has the power to annihilate His foes as well as the power to inflame the hearts of His followers with a personal love so strong as to fight for Him unto martyrdom, as the history of the Church amply testifies. As we gaze upon His bleeding form we profess with tears of gratitude that He so loved us unto death. St. John furnishes the slogan for the combat and assures us of victory in the words: "And they overcame him by the blood of the Lamb." (*Apoc.* 12:11).

The refrain of Good Friday's soul-stirring melody, "Jesus Our Love Is Crucified," should ever find a responsive chord in our hearts. All our outward activity will avail us little unless we are animated by an intense personal love of Christ. This was the secret of the Apostolate of St. Paul: "We preach Christ crucified, unto the Jews indeed a stumblingblock, and unto the Gentiles foolishness." (*1 Cor.* 1:23). "For I judged not myself to know anything among you, but Jesus Christ, and Him crucified." (*1 Cor.* 1:2).

Our reward for following "this beautiful one in his robe" will be the Beatific Vision in Heaven. "After this I saw great multitudes which no man could number. These are they who are come out of great tribulations, and have washed their robes and have made them white in the blood of the Lamb." (*Apoc.* 7:14). The "dyed garments from Bosra" will secure for us the white "Wedding Garment," which we will wear at the everlasting Marriage Supper of the Lamb.

Chapter 2

The Foreshadowing

G OD accepted Noe's sacrifice after the Deluge with complacency, but forbade him the use of blood. "Everything that moveth and liveth be meat for you: even as the green herb have I delivered them all to you: saving that flesh with blood ye shall not eat!" (*Gen.* 9:3-4).

Through Adam's act of disobedience man had fallen under the penalty of which God had forewarned him: "For in what day soever thou shalt eat of it, thou shalt die the death." (*Gen.* 2:17). After the flood Noe was to start a new life. He must not eat the blood which is the life, and as he poured it out upon the earth he would be reminded of his sin and punishment. The Divine command would create, or at least help to preserve, the impression of a lost life that was to be redeemed, and stimulate hope of the coming of the Messias who would restore all things.

Moses received the same command, and God gave him the reason for this prohibition of Blood: "I have given it to you, that you may make atonement with it upon the altar for your souls, and the blood may be for an expiation of the soul." (*Lev.* 17:11).

Why, then, was blood held so sacred? How could the blood of animals offered upon the altar become so pleasing to God? St. John Chrysostom answers: "God caused

10

it to be held sacred and considered Himself honored by it, not simply because it was blood, but because it represented, in type, the Blood of Jesus Christ."

As a pledge of His special protection to the Israelites in Egypt, God expressly chose the blood of the paschal lamb, the type of the true Lamb of God. "And the blood shall be unto you for a sign in the houses where you shall be: and I shall see the blood, and shall pass over you: and the plague shall not be upon you to destroy you." (*Ex.* 12:13).

Moses sealed the Old Covenant with sacrificial blood. "He took the blood and sprinkled it upon the people, and he said: 'This is the blood of the covenant which the Lord hath made with you concerning all these words.'" (*Ex.* 24:8).

The pouring out and sprinkling of the blood of animals, as types of "the Lamb of God that takes away the sins of the world," was one of the chief forms of worship in the Old Law for thousands of years. Blood enters into the very nature of sacrifice, for "the life of all flesh is in the blood." (*Lev.* 17:14); and again, "the blood is for the soul." (*Deut.* 12:23). Hence the reason for saying that devotion to the Precious Blood is as old as the world.

One of the principal rites of the bloody sacrifices of the Old Law was the laying of hands upon the victim's head and the shedding of its blood. By the former, the transferring of sins from the person offering to the animal offered, was symbolized, so that the victim, instead of the offender, might suffer the penalty of sin, which is death. The blood was offered to signify the life of the sinner, forfeited by sin.

The typical nature of these rites is sufficiently clear. Our sins were transferred to Christ, as Isaias says: "He hath borne our infirmities and carried our sorrows: he was wounded for our iniquities, he was bruised for our sins." (*Is.* 53:4). In the Holy Sacrifice of the Mass Our Lord offers Himself as a victim for our iniquities and sheds His Blood mystically, for the remission of sins.

One of these sacrifices of expiation is mentioned in the book of *Leviticus:* "And he shall put his hand upon the head thereof: and when he hath immolated it in the place where the holocaust is wont to be slain before the Lord, because it is for sin, the priest shall dip his finger in the Blood of the victim for sin, touching therewith the horns of the altar of holocaust, and pouring out the rest at the foot thereof." (*Lev.* 4:24-25).

According to St. Paul, Christ "by his own blood, entered once (forever) into the holies, having obtained (by his bloody death) eternal redemption. For if the blood of goats and oxen, sanctify such as are defiled, how much more shall the blood of Christ cleanse our conscience." (*Heb.* 9:11-14). Christ as a holocaust pouring out His Blood upon the altar of the cross is a victim infinitely more valuable than all the countless holocausts of Juda.

The bloody sacrifices of the Old Law, as prototypes, most certainly imply a sacrifice of blood in the New Dispensation. Hence St. Paul says: "Neither was the first (testament) indeed dedicated without blood. And almost all things, according to the law, are cleansed with blood: and without shedding of blood there is no remission." (*Heb.* 9:18-22).

"On the eve of the Passion as Christ sat with His disciples at the Last Supper, He took bread and broke it and said, 'This is My Body,' and He took wine and poured it out saying, 'This is My Blood of the new Covenant which shall be shed for you and for many unto the remission of sins; drink ye all of it.' And His disciples, brought up as they had been under the law, might have looked amazed. Drink the Blood. Why, the

Blood is the life, and the law forbade them to drink it. But the time to renew all things had come; the years of waiting were at an end. The woman's seed was there to give back in all its fullness the life that had been forfeited by disobedience. 'For this is the testimony that God hath given unto us eternal life, and this Life is in His Son; He that hath the Son hath Life, and he that hath not the Son hath not Life.'

"'Except therefore ye eat my flesh and drink my blood, ye have no life in you.' The Blood of the second Adam shed and given to him was at once to nourish and remind him of that new Life."—Maturin.

Chapter 3

The Rosy Dawn

TRULY could the Blessed Virgin Mary say of herself: I am the mystic vine which produced the sweet and lovely grape from which that mysterious wine of salvation was pressed, the Blood of the new and eternal Testament. "As the vine I have brought forth a pleasant odor; and my flowers are the fruit of honor and riches." (*Ecclus.* 24:23).

When God said to the serpent in the garden of Eden: "I will put enmities between thee and the woman, and thy seed and her seed," may we not conclude that He referred to the redeeming Blood of Jesus, assumed from the Immaculate Virgin Mary? "And they overcame him by the blood of the Lamb." (*Apoc.* 12:11).

Is not, then, the Immaculate Conception of the Blessed Virgin Mary, the morning star, and the Precious Blood of her Divine Son the roseate dawn of a new spiritual day? These are the two sweet memories of paradise lost, the recollection of which sheds a tender luster over this accursed earth: The Virgin, promised four thousand years before her birth, and the "Lamb slain from the beginning of the world." St. Hildegarde in her revelations, speaks of Our Lady as the morning dawn, because she hid in her womb the Blood of Our Saviour which casts forth rays of light.

Fallen man must be restored to the image of God,

and for this purpose the Son of God "emptied himself, taking the form of a servant, being made in the likeness of men, and in habit found as a man." (*Phil.* 2:7). But in the eternal wisdom of God it was decreed that without the effusion of Blood there would be no remission of sin, no restoration of man to the sonship of God. Blood had been flowing for over four thousand years, at the express command of God, as an acceptable homage to the Deity. The blood of animals, however, was only a type of the Blood of the Lamb of God; for nothing but a divine victim can appease the Divinity.

The Son of God, then, seeks a mother here upon earth. He asks for blood from the veins of a daughter of Adam, that He may belong to the human race. "Therefore because the children are partakers of flesh and blood, he also himself in like manner hath been partaker of the same." (*Heb.* 2:14). The great Archangel Gabriel is sent as the heavenly envoy to convey the message of this astounding mystery, and to whom? To a maiden who, in the eyes of the world, is but the bride of a laboring man. But she is a virgin without spot, whom God has enriched with every grace, and whose soul is a reflection of the Divine Purity.

"Hail, full of grace, the Lord is with thee," the Archangel speaks, and Mary replies: "Behold the handmaid of the Lord; be it done to me according to thy word." "And the word was made flesh."

"Bright as the blood of Adam, when the breath of God sent it sparkling through his veins, pure as the flesh of Eve, while standing yet in the mold of the Almighty's hands, as they drew it from the side of the slumbering man, were the blood and the flesh which the Spirit of God formed into the glorious humanity that Mary gave to Jesus"—Wiseman.

"The Precious Blood of Jesus flowing through His veins while an infant in His Holy Mother's womb, was derived from Mary. He lived with her life. She furnished from her Immaculate body the Precious Blood that Jesus shed for us. How close must have been the union of Jesus and Mary! Can we wonder at her surpassing holiness when she not only carried God within her womb, but furnished the very Body with which His Humanity clothes itself?

"We also find in this thought a fresh proof of Mary's unblemished purity. It is repugnant in our reverence for the Second Person of the Blessed Trinity to imagine Him dwelling in a womb that had ever been defiled with sin, or to suppose that the Precious Blood that flowed in His veins and was the price of our redemption did not come from a source as pure as God could make it.

"We must also remember that Jesus' Blood was wholly Mary's. It was not as in the case of other children who have an earthly father. The Body of Jesus was formed in Mary's womb by the operation of the Holy Ghost, and naturally Jesus was altogether hers. In Heaven, the Body that Jesus wears is still the Body derived from Mary, and this union is now closer than ever."— Clarke, S. J.

"In making the blood of His Son the price and vehicle of every grace, God has shown wonderful knowledge of the mysteries of human nature—if one could use these words with regard to One who has made human nature.

"Our blood is our human individuality. We are what we are through the communication of the blood of our parents. Our far-reaching differences of temperament and power come from the blood that flows in our veins. It makes us of what nature we are: apt for good, or prone to evil.

"Neither the philosopher nor the theologian can lay too much stress on the phenomena of heredity—

phenomena that invariably point to the fact that it is man's blood that contains the germs of parental depravities or perfections.

"In the Blood of the Son of God we have a blood of absolute human purity—a Blood that carries no germs of evil, but is filled through the human laws of heredity, with every perfection because it is Blood from an Immaculate Mother.

"The Blood of Our Lord is precious, primarily on account of Mary's spotlessness, through the immunity from all concupiscence, which was our Lady's privilege. That Our Lord's Blood should have been endowed with absolute purity we owe to Mary. Had she had the seeds of sin in her Blood, the *'fomes peccati'*, Our Lord's Blood might still have received purity from above; but it would not have had human purity, it would not have been precious as a human blood.

"But now, thanks to Mary's spotlessness, human blood flowed in the veins of our Lord that came down from Adam, and had nothing in itself except what was purest and noblest in the human race from the beginning.

"Besides this accumulation of human perfections, the Blood of Our Lord was made still more precious through the indwelling of the Spirit of God. It had divine heredity besides human heredity. The Spirit of God had filled it with the fullness of Divine Life, when it was already precious as the product of Mary's noble life.

"In this twofold heredity we have the key to the mystery of the Precious Blood; we know now why both its atoning and sanctifying power are infinite."

The Precious Blood is the fountain of the plenitude of all graces in Mary; it is also the source of her power to help us. Since Our Saviour constituted His Blessed Mother, standing beneath the Cross, the universal heiress of all the riches of His Blood, and since it is through her hands that we draw graces from the Saviour's fountains, is it not fitting that we should offer this same Precious Blood to God, through the hands of His Mother, for ourselves and for others?

The Blessed Curé of Ars, who was beatified only a few weeks later than Blessed Gaspar del Bufalo, the great promoter of the devotion to the Precious Blood, says: "Accustom yourselves to the following efficacious manner of prayer: ask the Blessed Virgin to offer to the Heavenly Father her Divine Son all covered with Blood and wounds for the conversion of sinners. This is a most excellent prayer. My children, remember this well. I never failed to obtain any grace that I asked of God in this manner."

Oh, what a powerful prayer, what a merciful and irresistible pleading, when the Mother of God offers by her immaculate hands, the redemptive Blood of Calvary, the Eucharistic Blood of the Mass, in our behalf for the conversion of sinners, for the propagation of the faith, for the sick and dying, and for the souls in Purgatory!

Who could better imbue us with a love of the Blood of our Redemption than the Sorrowful Mother whose heartbeats stimulated the growth of this Sacred Blood, she, who saw it shed seven times, saw it rudely trampled under foot by Jew and Gentile and mixed with the mire of this accursed earth, she, whose lips were reddened by kissing the wounds of the Crucified—how she must long to see the devotion to this Precious Blood spread over the entire world, and reach every heart! With what love she watches those who follow in her footsteps, in making atonement to the Blood of our Redemption.

Thy immaculate heart, O Blessed Virgin Mary, Mother of God, was the virginal source of the Precious Blood of my Redeemer. It is, then, the fountainhead of my salvation. With filial love, with deepest gratitude and with unbounded confidence, I cry to thee: "Sweet Heart of Mary, be my salvation!"

Eve offered us the fruit of death; but thou, O most Holy Mother, didst give us the fruit of eternal life. How can I thank thee enough, for so sublime a gift? O my celestial Queen, how could I ever forget thee? How could I but love thee! Forever and ever thou shalt be to me "the mother of fair love, and of fear, and of knowledge, and of holy hope."

Chapter 4

This Beautiful One In His Robe

The Crucifixion

JESUS is come to save His people from their sins; "without shedding of Blood there is no remission of sin." He is come to conquer sin and death; and this is why "His garment is sprinkled with Blood" from first to last—from swaddling clothes to shroud. The purpose of His coming is to take away the sins of the world; it is declared today when His name is called Jesus, and it is made all the more evident when that most Holy Name is steeped in His Precious Blood, enriched with those ruby drops. He is come to save sinners; and so from the first He puts on the form of a sinner, will be treated as one, and therefore fulfills all justice by this baptism of Blood—as later on He will receive John's baptism of water. Therefore, the child is circumcised; that is, the sinless Saviour submits to the appointed rite whereby the forgiveness of original sin is conveyed to the souls of His people, until His new rite and more perfect Sacrament of Baptism shall displace it. "When He cometh into the world, He saith: 'Sacrifice and oblation Thou wouldst not: but a body Thou hast given me.' Then said I, 'Behold, I come to do Thy will, O God.'" But how does He say this? Does this Infant speak? Ah, no. Those lovely lips utter no word, and though the Babe is the Word of God, He is unheard. Still, the Infant saith the predicted words: for He speaks with "the voice of Blood," and the Blood of the Babe of Bethlehem "speaks better things than the Blood of Abel." He knows that He actually lies on the straw of the stable's manger, and like a little lamb, He will offer these Blood-drops of the Circumcision as a pledge of the total shedding of His Blood when He shall come to die on Calvary.

Love of Christ! Who shall measure thee? Impatient to begin the Bloodsheddings, reluctant to leave off! The first and the last unnecessary for our redemption, yet necessary to Thy prodigal generosity!

The Agony in the Garden

The second Bloodshedding took place in the olive garden of Gethsemani; and devout souls are summoned thither to behold the drops of Blood trickling down upon the ground. "I am come into my garden, my spouse, I have gathered my myrrh." (*Cant.* 5:1). He Who "did no sin" begins to feel sadness, dejection and fear. Grief oppresses Him, woe transfigures Him and transforms His very features. He clothes Himself with shame and sorrow, as He might put on the garb of a criminal, being about to die a criminal's death. And thus He appears before His Father, fearful and ashamed—the Penitent, the Man of Sorrows—and with love and deep contrition, full of pain and heart-breaking anguish, He falls prostrate, and in mental sadness hides His sacred face upon the ground. Tomorrow His body will be fastened, motionless and bleeding, on the Cross; now, it is His soul that is wounded and crucified. The sorrows of death, its chills, and its clammy sweat inundate the prostrate form of Jesus. "My soul is sorrowful even unto death!" "O earth, earth, earth, hear the word of the Lord." (*Jer.* 22:29). "O earth, cover not my blood." (*Job* 16:19). His agony increases, He is "poured out like water" (*Ps.* 21:15), only the plenteous sweat is no longer like water, but "like drops of blood trickling on the ground." His head is "filled with dew, and His locks with the dews of night"—only, His head and whole body are bedewed and drenched with Blood. Blood oozes from every pore; His long garments are soaked with Blood; the thick woolen texture cannot absorb it, the cold night air cannot clot it; it gushes forth again and again, at the throbs and beats of His agonized Heart, and trickles, ever trickles, to the ground, till He is lying in a pool of blood. "I have trodden the winepress alone." (*Is.* 63:3).

The Scourging

Two of the soldiers place themselves on either side of Jesus; the crowd falls back to give them room; the garments, whose very fringe gives health, are trampled under foot; the hands that have bestowed blessings, and alms, and absolutions are bound; and the shoulders of the Good Shepherd, where His lost sheep will be laid so lovingly, and carried so gently, await the first stroke of the scourge.

In an instant the rods are raised; there is a shrill sound as the air is cut; then a sharp, loud report, as though something cracks or breaks. Alas! It is the first blow on the shoulders of Christ, as the red Blood springs out to testify. The frame of Jesus quivers, for it is exquisitely sensitive; but His face remains unchanged. Again and again they strike, more and more recklessly, maddened by the patient calmness of that uplifting countenance. "I have been scourged all the day." (*Ps.* 72:14). "The wicked hath wrought upon my back, they have prolonged their iniquity." (*Ps.* 128:3). "For I am ready

for scourges, and my sorrow is continually before me"—
His sorrow for our sins. So, with a new sound, that
startles the ears of His horrified Mother, the whistling
cords sweep from right to left, from left to right, to be
embedded in mangled flesh. Blood pours from the
widening wounds. Sometimes it falls heavily and slowly
on the pavement, like the big drops of rain before thun-
der; sometimes, it is heard fast-dripping and trickling
like the shower from the eaves of houses, or the water
from the roofs of rocky caves. There lies the long white
whips of steel-like sinews—these are seized. The Victim is paler, His lips are parched and cracked, and
parted to breathe the hot air. His tongue is swollen—
He nerves and steadies Himself for what is to come.
Still more rejoicingly does the dear Blood of God leap
forth. He looks like one frayed alive, whose flesh is cut
to shreds. Finally, the fastenings are severed, and Jesus
falls into a pool of His own Blood, then slowly rises to
His knees, and with excruciating suffering draws the
seamless tunic over His mangled flesh, and conceals
the fearful evidence of their cruelty and of His own
brave, generous love.

The Crowning With Thorns

Terrible as were the ruffians when in earnest, they
are more terrible in their jest. Conceive the torture,
when the head of Jesus is seized, held with rough,
irreverent grasp, and then encircled and fitted with a
crown—not of flowers, but—alas!—of sharpest thorns.
Careful not to hurt themselves, they are callous to His
anguish, and heedless of the hot Blood which gushes
out over their hands and garments. But we must watch
every drop; for this is the beginning of the Fourth
Bloodshedding.

Blood pours down the face and neck of Jesus. Blood

reddens the green crown; beads of Blood hang like berries upon its spikes. Blood fastens and glues together the long locks that fall on His shoulders. Blood drops on the tattered, faded cloak, and dyes it a purple that is truly royal and divine. Blood crimsons the bench which serves for a throne, and the wall and the marble pavement around His feet. But His brutal tormentors care not either for His Blood or His pain. They only mock more rudely and savagely, as they thrust into His patient hand the reed-sceptre, and begin the dastardly outrage of their mock homage and adoration. O Man of Sorrows, with Thy beautiful countenance hidden and despised, in faith and love we bend the knee and adore. We hail Thee, King of Kings!

"Jesus came forth, bearing the crown of thorns and the purple garment!" Pilate, in a last effort to save Him from the Jews, brings Him forth that all may see and pity Him. "Behold the Man!" And still the red Blood gathers on the thorns, and it falls on the pavement where He stands; and the crown grows redder: nor king, nor emperor has ever worn one so royal, so rich, so precious. The Evangelists tell us that when they took Jesus and led Him forth, the purple garment was taken from Our Lord and replaced by His own, but they do not mention any removal of the crown of thorns. He kept it, and so went forth to die. His Mother saw that death-garland upon the Victim's brow, when He halted before her on the road to the place of sacrifice.

The Way of the Cross

The history of the Passion of Our Lord is written in His Precious Blood; and even in the passing from pain to pain, one of the Bloodsheddings take place.

The soldiers take their purple garment off Our Lord and clothe Him again in His own. But why does the

Precious Blood, which has been falling so fast and plenteously, now hide itself out of sight? The purple robe was soaked with it and dyed anew; and, unlike His own garment—being rent and ragged—it covered but few of His bleeding wounds—and now so little of that Blood is seen! Ah, the Precious Blood has been misunderstood, has been blasphemed. By a miracle of malice, they have changed God's richest blessing into a dreadful anathema—they have taken the Blood of Christ on themselves and on their unhappy children; they have invoked their own reprobation and damnation.

The first Blood which moistens the Cross is that left by the lips of Jesus: for He gives it a kind and gentle kiss of peace, a divine reconciliation He will effect between justice and mercy. "This is he that came by water and blood," (*1 Jn.* 5:6). He comes to us by Blood, for through the weight of the Cross His many wounds are made to bleed afresh: at every step, Blood gushes from His veins; it steals down beneath the garments till it bathes His faltering feet, till it reaches the ground, to be trampled on and hidden in dust and sand. And yet it will not be wholly hidden; for it has a purpose, this Bloodshedding of the Way of the Cross. The path is now being marked out by which the Kingdom of Heaven must be stormed. Up this toilsome road the soldiers of the Lord are to press on till doomsday, following their Captain and King.

O fainting, feeble, bleeding Cross-bearer! How wilt Thou accomplish Thy task of beating down the gates of Hell, and setting wide for the Blessed gates of Paradise—Thou who seemest too weak to perform even the least part thereof, too exhausted to carry that Cross any further on the road? "*In Sanguine Meo*"—"In My Blood."

The Crucifixion

"Jesus, that He might sanctify the people with His own blood, suffered without the gate." (*Heb.* 13:12). The executioners order Him to go to the Cross and place Himself upon it, that they might see where to make the holes to receive the nails. This mark is not necessary; no golden reed for measurement is needed here, for His own Blood has itself marked out all the length and breadth that His body and arms will require. Until death part them, He will not leave His Cross, not even when they dare Him to come down; for see how He has embraced it, and testified His love by endowing it with these rich, ruby jewels of His Most Precious Blood!

And now a soldier selects a nail; it is long and strong, but neither smooth nor sharp-pointed. Slowly and deliberately he puts the nail upon the palm of the open hand of Jesus. In spirit, Mary kisses that gracious hand, which she will never again see, as for three and thirty years she has seen it, without a wound. They have dug into His left hand, they have opened the first of the Saviour's Five Fountains, but the Blood of Redemption comes only slowly forth past the great nail and the bruised lips of the wound. The ready right hand is fitted with another huge spike, and this with repeated blows is also struck into the quivering nerves and muscles. The soldiers now seize the sacred feet, and through both a long nail, by dint of redoubled blows, is sent on its crashing, rending way into the Cross. Four Fountains now are dug, and Jesus is crucified. The red Blood pours out rejoicingly, and running down from hands and feet, bathes alike both Crucified and Cross.

For three long hours the Saving Stream flows on, at one time slowly, as the chills and langor of death prevail, at another time fast and hot, as the love of the Sacred Heart urges it forth. Its very panting assists the Sixth Bloodshedding. Even as in His Divinity Jesus has "emptied Himself" to take this form of ours, so in generous emulation will His Human Nature empty itself and pour out every drop of its Life-blood like water in Jerusalem. O Redeemer, we accept Thy boon—but we receive it weeping.

The Piercing of the Sacred Heart

Is it not enough that the Lamb of God is slain? To attack the body of Jesus is to crucify Him again, "to trample under foot the Son of God, and to esteem the blood of the Testament unclean." (*Heb.* 10:29). One of the soldiers raises a spear and thrusts it violently into the dead body of Jesus. So savagely is the spear-thrust given, that the side of Our Lord is opened and the Sacred Heart is pierced, "and immediately there came forth blood and water." The Fifth Fountain of the Saviour is dug—it is the Seventh Bloodshedding. Naturally, no result would have followed this stroke of the lance, which God in His patience permitted and did not punish on the spot. Naturally, a corpse so scourged, so wounded, would have no Blood left in its vein. Naturally, even were there some few drops in life's final stronghold, the heart, they would not flow when life was ended. But behold! Blood, bright, red, glorious and triumphant Blood leaps forth—and not Blood alone, but water, pure, fresh and sparkling water comes forth. It is true Blood, it is true water—a portent and prodigy, a miracle so astounding, that in relating it the Evangelist reminds us he was there, an eyewitness, and he is inspired to pledge his personal veracity in attestation of the mysterious event. He sees the sacred body, and well may he think that every drop of the Precious Blood is shed. Like mountain springs and streams in the burning summer-tide, each Fountain of the Saviour is dry, and the red Blood darkens and hardens round the edge of His wounds and the seams of the scourging. Yet Jesus is not content. For, now in death, the holy head of Jesus bends down toward His side, as if to point out more of His treasures. No one could dream that He who has been so prodigal still has treasures left—a sealed and secret Fountain, a hidden store of sweetest Blood to bestow after death as a legacy of love. Dearest Lord! Thy last miracle is like Thy first— "Thou hast kept the best wine until now." (*John* 2:10). "You shall draw waters with joy out of the Saviour's Fountain." (*Is.* 12:3). Thus are the Seven Bloodshed-dings completed, thus is prophecy fulfilled.—An extract from *The Blood of the Lamb* by Digby Best.

Chapter 5

Why Is Thy Apparel Red?

THE magnificent temple, the hundreds of priests and levites, the solemn rites, the beautiful songs, the thousands of victims—all this in the Jewish worship—was inspiring indeed. That, however, which must have made the deepest impression on the faithful Israelites was seeing the priest who had charge of the temple service accept and slay the offering, carefully gather its blood, sprinkle with it him who offered the victim, and pour out the remainder around the altar. This was a daily custom, and lasted from the time of Aaron to the coming of Christ, with the exception of the period during which the Jews were in captivity.

What a unique scene is presented to our vision in the description of the ceremonies of the Passover, the greatest feast of the Hebrews, in which they celebrated their escape from the angel of the Passover, and their deliverance from Egyptian bondage! In commemoration of these miraculous events, Moses commanded that at Eastertide a lamb be slain by every family and the doorpost sprinkled three times with its blood. In the days of Christ it was customary for every Jew to eat the paschal lamb at Jerusalem. The city itself was not large enough to contain the immense number of guests; they therefore pitched their tents beyond the city limits. Josephus tells us that just before the destruction of Jerusalem 250,000 lambs were slain at one time for the feast of Easter. Since no fewer than ten persons partook of each lamb, we can estimate the number of persons who participated in this grand act of sacrifice.

When we recall the manner in which these sacrificial lambs were immolated, the scene becomes still more spectacular. At three o'clock on the Thursday before Easter, the priests of the temple blew great blasts on their silver trumpets to tell the waiting multitude that they were ready for the sacrifice of the paschal lamb. Then hundreds of thousands of lambs came into view, carried hither and thither from the temple, on the shoulders of the leader of each little band of pilgrims. Each lamb was then suspended on two sticks forming a cross. The longer stick was driven through the body and into the tendons of the hind leg; the shorter one caused the front feet to be extended. These supports were of wood. In this manner the lamb was roasted, and placed upon the table. What a true image of Our Lord on the Cross! Think of one-fourth of a million lambs extended on such cross-sticks! Picture to your mind the blood of these lambs on a hundred thousand doorposts, between which the Jews passed, as between so many signs of God's merciful promises. "The blood shall be unto you for a sign in the houses where you shall be and I shall see the blood, and shall pass over you." (*Ex.* 12:13). Verily, Jerusalem was in that day a city of crosses and blood and sacrificial lambs. This was the feast of the Pasch celebrated for hundreds of years by the faithful Hebrews. Was there no special meaning, or deep significance in all this?

What a grand spectacle in the sight of high Heaven, looking down upon this sinful earth, to behold now, not 250,000 sacrificial lambs and the bloody doorposts of the Old Law, but Jesus the Son of the living God, "a Lamb standing as it were slain," (*Apoc.* 5:6) on two hundred and fifty thousand altars, in the Holy Sacrifice of the Mass, every day, the world over, pleading with His five wounds for us "poor banished children of Eve!" Two hundred and fifty thousand chalices with Thy Blood, O Lord, the Blood of Gethsemani, of the Pretorium, of Golgatha—all the Blood poured out in Thy seven effusions! What love, what a bountiful redemption! *"Copiosa apud eum redemptio."* (*Ps.* 129). The Hebrew high-priest entered once in the long round of twelve months the dread Holy of Holies in the great Temple of old, holding on high before his eyes a chalice of steaming blood. Now hundreds of thousands of priests ascend the altar daily to hold aloft for our propitiation the chalice containing, not the blood of an animal, but the adorable Blood of the Son of God.

The divine Blood issuing from the Saviour's sacred wounds on Calvary was destined to flow over the entire earth, for all time to come, through the Church which our Redeemer established in His Blood. "He hath purchased the Church with His own Blood." (*Acts* 20:28). God the Father sent a deluge of water to destroy all living creatures. During Holy Week the Church sings: *"Terra, pontus, astra, mundus quo lavantur flumine."* "The earth, the sea, the stars, the whole world, have been washed in this flood." The Church also sings in her office, *"Mira tandem vis amoris, lavit orbem flumine."* "The marvelous strength of love has washed the universe with this Blood." More beautiful than the rivers of Paradise, this life-giving stream flows through the channels of the Mass and the Sacraments, into millions of hearts—purifying, sanctifying and glorifying souls. Every good thought and every holy desire taking root in the heart and blossoming into fruit, issues from a soil that has been moistened by the Precious Blood.

"And I, if I be lifted up from the earth, will draw
all things to myself." (*John* 12:32). But how wilt thou
draw us, O Lord? Ah, as the flower is inclined to the
sun, as the hart is drawn to the running fountain! By
the love of Thy Precious Blood leaping out from Thy
Sacred Heart on the Cross, and falling in profusion
over us, in the Holy Sacrifice of the Mass, and flowing through the channels of Thy Sacrament into our
souls, thereby softening our hardened hearts and reviving our indifferent and drooping spirits, as plants after
a refreshing rain. "But now in Christ Jesus, you, who
some time were afar off, are made nigh by the Blood
of Christ." (*Eph.* 2:13). "The Blood of Christ is a mag-
net that draws souls unto itself and inclines God, the
tree of life, to show His mercy."—St. Mary Magdalen
de Pazzi.

"The shedding of Christ's Blood on the Cross is
renewed in the Mass. Once for all Christ shed His
Blood in a visible and painful manner, but at this we
could not be present. This shedding of Blood is, however, repeated daily in an invisible manner. St. Chrysostom says: "The Lamb of God is immolated for thee, His
Blood flows mystically upon the altar; the Blood contained in the chalice is drawn for thy cleansing from
His sacred side."

"In the formula of consecration the priest does not
content himself with saying: 'This is the chalice of My
Blood;' he continues, by using Christ's own words: 'which
shall be shed for you and for many, to the remission
of sins.' As the first part of the sentence is certainly
fulfilled, with no less certainty will the latter part be
fulfilled. Consequently the sacred Blood of Christ is
verily and indeed shed in the Mass."—Cochem.

This same author proceeds as follows: "As the Precious Blood is really shed when Mass is celebrated, so
it is likewise sprinkled upon all who are present, and

poured out upon their souls. Of this we have a clear type in the Old Testament, to which St. Paul refers when he speaks of how Moses sprinkled the blood of calves and goats upon all the people, saying: 'This is the blood of the testament, which God hath enjoined unto you.' (*Heb.* 9:20). The words Christ employed when He consecrated the chalice at the Last Supper, are almost identical: 'This is the new testament in my Blood.' (*Luke* 22:20). St. Paul adds, in the passage already quoted: 'It is necessary, therefore, that the patterns of heavenly things should be cleansed with these: but the heavenly things themselves with better sacrifices than these.' By this he meant to say that the Jewish synagogue, which was a type of the Catholic Church, was cleansed by the sprinkling of the blood of calves and goats, whereas the Catholic Church is cleansed by the Blood of the Lamb of God.

"St. Chrysostum says: 'Thou seest that Christ is immolated in the Mass, thou seest that the people present are sprinkled and marked with the crimson Blood from His veins.' In this passage this great doctor of the Church expressly asserts that in Holy Mass the Blood of Christ is not merely poured out *for* us, but poured out *upon* us. Marchantius says the same: 'The Precious Blood is shed in the Mass as a holy oblation, and the souls of the faithful who stand around are sprinkled with it.'

"St. Paul speaks very clearly: 'You are come to Jesus the mediator of the New Testament, and to the sprinkling of blood which speaketh better than that of Abel.' (*Heb.* 12:24). Here it may be asked: When do we come to Jesus, our mediator? In Holy Communion we approach very near to Him, and receive Him into our hearts. But we do not come to Him as to our mediator then: we receive Him as our spiritual sustenance. It is in Holy Mass that we come to Him as our true mediator and intercessor, for in this He is Himself the real high priest, whose office it is to make intercession for the people. Now if we come to Him in the Mass as to our mediator, at the same time we come, as St. Paul says, 'to the sprinkling of blood.' This sprinkling takes place whenever Mass is celebrated; our bodies are not sprinkled, but our souls. In His passion the Blood of Christ was shed, but it fell upon the stones and upon the ground. In Holy Mass the self-same Blood is shed; it does not, however, fall upon the earth, nor upon the bodies of men: it is applied to the souls of those who are present. Just as Moses sprinkled the Jews with the blood of the sacrificial victims, and the priest sprinkles Christian people with holy water, so Christ spiritually sprinkles the souls of the faithful with His blood, which is shed for them in the Mass.

"This spiritual sprinkling is far more beneficial to us than the material sprinkling. Hear what St. Magdalen of Pazzi says concerning it: 'This blood, when applied to the soul, imparts to it as much dignity as if it were decked in a costly robe; it imparts to it such brilliancy and splendor that couldst thou behold the effulgence of thy soul when sprinkled with that blood thou wouldst fall down to adore it.' Remarkable words indeed! Happy the soul which is adorned with such beauty! Go often to Mass, dear reader, that thou mayest there be sprinkled with the Blood of Christ arrayed in rich apparel, which will render thee glorious forever in the sight of angels and saints." We here recall the words of the Prophet spoken of Christ: "Who is this that cometh from Edom, with dyed garments from Bosra? This beautiful one in his robe, walking in the greatness of his strength . . . Why then is thy apparel red, and thy garments like theirs that tread in the winepress?" (*Is.* 63:1).

We have seen that the Blood of Christ is shed for

us and that our souls are sprinkled with it in the Mass. Now we must not forget that this sacred Blood cries to God in the Holy Sacrifice and ascends to His throne as an odor of sweetness in our behalf.

"Although the cry sent up by innumerable sins is so loud that it is heard in the high Heaven, yet the voice of the Blood of Christ pleading for us in the Holy Sacrifice of the Mass is still more powerful; it is almighty and infinite; it does not merely pierce the clouds, it reaches the heart of God the Father. God said to Cain: 'The voice of thy brother's blood crieth to me from the earth.' (*Gen.* 4:10). If the blood of innocent Abel cried from the ground with so loud a voice that it was heard in Heaven, and God Himself was compelled to look down from Heaven upon the earth, and avenge the fratricidal act, what will not the power of Christ's Blood be, shed as it is daily upon our altars, and offered up to God! Abel's blood cried for vengeance; the Blood of Christ cries for mercy. Now we know that God is far more inclined to show mercy than to do vengeance; as the Church says in one of her prayers: 'O God, whose property is ever to have mercy and to spare.' The voice of Abel's blood was no audible voice, yet it was so powerful that it rose from earth to Heaven. The voice of the Blood shed by Jesus Christ in Holy Mass is likewise mystic, yet it, too, is so powerful that it compels an angry God to show mercy. 'You are come to Jesus the mediator of the New Testament, and to the sprinkling of blood, which speaketh better than that of Abel.' This passage implies that if we come to Jesus, sprinkled with blood, that blood cries to God for mercy upon sinners with a voice that will take no denial.

"In addition to the all-prevailing cry which the Blood of Christ sends up to Heaven, there is something else peculiar to it, whereby the anger of God is appeased; namely, the sweet odor which ascends from that Blood when it is shed upon the altar. Referring to the Jewish burnt-sacrifice, God says: 'The morning holocaust you shall always offer every day of the seven days for the food of the fire, and for a most sweet odor to the Lord, which shall rise from the holocaust, and from the libations of each.' (*Num.* 28:23, 24). Now if the odor arising from the burnt flesh of animals and the effusion of their blood was agreeable to Almighty God, what will not the most sweet odor of Christ's precious blood effect, when offered upon the altar as a holocaust worthy of His divine majesty!

"When the priest offers the chalice, he says: 'We offer unto Thee, O Lord, the chalice of salvation, beseeching Thy clemency, that in the sight of Thy divine majesty it may ascend with the odor of sweetness for our salvation, and for that of the whole world!' The priest makes use of these words because the wine contained in the chalice will be changed into the precious blood of Christ. St. Paul says: 'Christ hath loved us, and hath delivered Himself for us, an oblation, and a sacrifice to God for an odor of sweetness.' (*Eph.* 5:2). When this precious holocaust was offered upon the cross, with shedding of Blood and at the cost of great pain, so delicious was the fragrance that ascended to Heaven that it counteracted the evil odor that arose from the many and grievous sins of mankind. For the death of Christ, the shedding of His Blood, was more pleasing to God than the iniquities of the world were displeasing to Him. And when this divine Victim is sacrificed and His Blood shed mystically upon our altars, a sweet and agreeable odor daily ascends thence unto the Lord. Thus, if with a contrite heart thou dost offer the Precious Blood of Christ to God in Holy Mass, not only dost thou dispel the stench of thy sins by the perfume of His Blood, but thou dost more to please God than thou hast done to displease Him by thy misdeeds."

God the Father did not take pleasure in seeing His Divine Son dripping Blood amidst excruciating torments. That was naturally abhorrent to Him. But in as much as it was Love suffering, Love pleading and Love bleeding as a Victim for the sins of mankind, Jesus was to His Heavenly Father also "this beautiful one in his robe."

The Sacrifice of the Mass, although called an unbloody sacrifice, is nevertheless a renewal of the Sacrifice of the Cross and a memorial of our Lord's Passion and Death. At the Elevation, therefore, we may view Him in the vision of Isaias, who contemplated Him in the red apparel of His Blood.

Fr. McNabb writes in his characteristic way: "Every morning before God goes out to see and to judge the crowded sins of the world, He turns His eyes towards the out-stretched arms of Jesus; and the scent of the new-fallen Blood changes His righteous wrath into a more righteous mercy."

"When the patriarch Isaac, whose eyes were dimmed with age, had kissed his son Jacob, dressed in the garments of his brother Esau, Holy Scripture tells us that on smelling the fragrant odor of his garments, he blessed him, and desired for him every kind of temporal prosperity. The most sweet odor of Christ's Blood has a similar effect; so that God looks with favor upon the pious worshipper who offers it to him in Holy Mass, and bestows upon him His divine benediction, with an increase of grace and of celestial gifts. All the saints, too, rejoice when Mass is celebrated, when the perfume of the sacred Blood rises in clouds of fragrance from the altar, filling the courts of Heaven, to the joy and refreshment of all its blessed inhabitants. Let it, therefore, be our endeavor when present at Mass to adore the precious blood with devout veneration, to implore its intercession, and to offer it to God for our salvation."

At this stream of Christ's Precious Blood, let us weep when we remember our Saviour's intense love for us, as did the Israelites of old when they remembered Sion near the rivers of Babylon. Let our "right hand be forgotten," if we do not hang up our work-a-day instruments to make the Holy Sacrifice of the New Law "the beginning of our joy," at least on the Lord's day. "Let my tongue cleave to my jaws," if I sound not Thy praise, O Lord, in Thy holy temple, where Thou, our King, dost offer worship to Thy heavenly Father in our behalf. For "you are come to Mount Sion, and to the city of the living God, the heavenly Jerusalem, and to the company of many thousands of angels and to Jesus the mediator of the New Testament, and to the sprinkling of blood which speaketh better than that of Abel." (*Heb.* 12:22-24).

Chapter 6

My Blood Is Drink Indeed

I N THE Gospel of St. John, Our Lord says: "Except you eat the flesh of the Son of man, and drink his blood, you shall not have life in you. He that eateth my flesh, and drinketh my blood, hath everlasting life: and I will raise him up in the last day. For my flesh is meat indeed. He that eateth my flesh, and drinketh my blood, abideth in me, and I in him." (*John* 6:54-57). It is plain, from these texts, that Our Lord wants us to partake of His Body and Blood, if we would have life in us.

However, we must never lose sight of the Catholic doctrine, that in Holy Communion Christ comes to us in person, and that the Body of Christ is now (after the resurrection) inseparable from His Personality, from His Blood, from His Soul, from His Divinity, so that wherever His Body is, there also is Christ, whole and entire. They do not receive the Blood of Christ in greater measure who receive under the form of wine alone, because whoever receives under any form receives not His Body only, nor the Blood only, but Christ Himself.

"With very good reason has it been ordained that two consecrations should take place in the Mass; first, to represent more effectively the Passion of our Lord, in which His Blood was separated from His Body, wherefore, in the consecration, we mention the effusion of

His Blood; and secondly, because, as the Sacrament was to be used by us to nurture the soul, it was most fitting that it should be instituted as meat and drink, which evidently constitute the perfect sustenance of the body.

"When, therefore, it is said in the words of the consecration: 'For this is the chalice of my blood,' these words are to be understood to mean: This is my blood, which is contained in this chalice. Rightly and appositely is mention of *'the chalice'* to be made at the consecration of the Blood, as it is the drink of the faithful; for the blood, were it not contained in some vessel, would not seem sufficiently to signify this sort of drink."—Catechism of the Council of Trent.

From the very fact that Our Lord Himself so often mentions His Blood separately from His Body, we may infer that he wishes us to think of His Blood, in Holy Communion particularly, as the drink of our souls, and that we should worship it in a special manner. "My blood is drink indeed."

"I am the Vine; you are the branches." "When Our Lord made use of this comparison, He had just instituted the Most Holy Eucharist, in which He had given His own Blood to His Apostles under the species of wine, and had left it to all the faithful until the end of the world—that all might drink of it in their turn, and thus by the virtue of that mystic Wine might become inflamed with the love of their Divine Master, and might be enabled courageously to overcome all temptations. Just as when the grape is crushed an exquisite and precious wine wells forth, so from the Lamb of God, pressed in the wine-press of the Cross, that precious Blood poured forth as the price of our redemption and as the life-giving potion of our soul!"

In Holy Communion we are not merely sprinkled with the Blood of Jesus; we actually draw immediately from the fountains themselves, and we can say with St. Cyprian: "We imbibe the Blood of Our Lord, and press our lips upon the wounds of Our Saviour." There was a time in the Church when the priest dipped his fingers into the species of wine and then applied the Precious Blood to the lips of newborn children, so that in this way they were able to receive the Sacrament.

"The Blood of Our Lord is drunk by our souls in the mystery of the Holy Eucharist, is drunk by that highest and innermost part of ourselves, where spiritual temperament, or conscience, is to be found; and it gives to that part of our being, by a new kind of heredity, its own nobility; it makes us have God in our blood.

"When you are in contact with a Catholic people, with Catholic multitudes (for masses are the best guide in these things), you find a refinement of thought, a depth of feeling in things spiritual, a keen insight into heavenly matters, which are painfully wanting in non-Catholic populations.

"You ask yourself why this gulf between the mental states of two families of people, geographically and racially perhaps, so near. There is only one answer possible: It is in the Blood—in the Blood that is drunk by the Catholic people, that has been drunk by their fathers and their father's fathers."—Dom. Anscar Vonier, O.S.B.

In Thy Divine Blood, O Jesus, there is life and love, light and joy; for it replenishes the lamp of faith with divine oil, causing the fire of hope and love to flame up high in our hearts, thereby reviving our waning courage and expanding our hearts so that we may run in the way of Thy Commandments.

"O Blood, to recall thee, is to restore light and heat to our cold and clouded souls! Hasten to melt our icy hearts and clouded souls! Hasten to melt our icy hearts, and enlighten our bedimmed sight. In the Blood of Thy Sacred Heart, O Lord, is the hidden fire that consumes our imperfections. In the Blood we find our mercy-source; in the Blood, clemency; in the Blood, fire; in the Blood, compassion."—St. Catherine of Siena.

Lord, I hear Thee asking me: "Can you drink of the chalice that I drink of?" I understand—it is the chalice of suffering which Thou dost offer Thy favorite ones in this life. "Behold they whose judgment was not to drink of the cup, shall certainly drink: and shalt thou come off as innocent?" (*Jer.* 49:12). Blood of Christ inebriates me, that the courage and fortitude of martyrs may animate my soul!

We can cause this Precious Blood to flow every moment in spiritual communion by faith and ardent desire, thus applying the merits of Christ more and more to our souls.

O Jesus, I long, I yearn, to love Thee with the transports of love with which those souls that are at this moment entering Heaven love Thee! O Jesus, give Thyself to me now in spiritual communion, as Thou art giving Thyself to them in Heaven!

O Sacred Blood, which flowed so copiously seven times for my salvation, I love Thee, I praise Thee, I adore Thee with ardent gratitude! The purest of fountains from which Thou didst flow, makes Thy memory so sweet! O Precious Blood, with trumpet tones Thou speakest to me of the love of my God and Redeemer! How I deplore my coldness and indifference towards Thee! Now, at last, I wish to return love for love; blood for blood, if need be. As often as my pulse beats, it shall beat for Thee, O my bleeding Jesus! Every drop of blood that passes through my heart shall greet Thee, Thou sweet guest of my soul, and shall return to the arteries, warmed and purified by Thy love. So long as the blood courses through my veins, it shall flow for love of Thee alone; it shall circulate only for Thy interest and shall turn cold and stand still only because I am about to love Thee in eternity. Oh, let this precious stream of Thy love flow through every heart and inebriate every soul with holy joy!

During the first centuries the priest or the deacon conveyed the chalice containing the consecrated wine to the lips of the faithful, who took a small quantity of it. In the Middle Ages use was made of a golden or silver tube through which the faithful used to draw and suck in the Precious Blood. The author of the Imitation alludes to this practice (Book 4, c. 4). During the same period the rite of communicating under both species underwent many changes. In some countries the priest poured some drops of consecrated wine into a large quantity of unconsecrated wine, and it was of the latter that the people partook at Holy Communion. In other countries the priest gave them the Sacred Host after it had been lightly dipped into the consecrated wine. However, the custom of distributing pure consecrated wine prevailed.

"By a law of Holy Church it has since been forbidden that anyone but the priests consecrating the Body of the Lord in the sacrifice should receive the Holy Eucharist under both kinds, without the authority of the Church itself. There are various and many reasons why the laity are not to communicate under both species. In the first place, the greatest caution was necessary to avoid spilling the Blood of the Lord on the ground, a thing that seemed not easy to be avoided, if the chalice ought to be administered to a large assemblage of the people. Besides, as the Holy Eucharist ought to be in readiness for the sick, it was very much to be apprehended where the species of wine long unconsumed, that it might turn acid. Moreover, there are very many who cannot at all bear the taste, or even the smell of wine; lest, therefore, what is intended for the health of the soul should prove noxious to the body, most prudently has it been enacted by the Church, that the faithful should receive the species of bread only. It is further to be observed that, in several countries, they labor under extreme scarcity of wine, nor can it be brought from elsewhere without very heavy expenses. In the next place, a circumstance most of all to the point, the heresy of those was to be uprooted, who denied that Christ, whole and entire, is contained under either species and asserted that the body only without the Blood is contained under the species of bread, and the Blood only under the species of wine. In order, therefore, that the truth of the Catholic faith might be placed more clearly before the eyes of all, communion under one kind, that is, under that of bread, was most wisely introduced."—Catechism of the Council of Trent.

Now that the frequent and daily reception of Holy Communion is more generally advocated and more widely practiced, the wisdom of the Church, in withholding the cup from the laity, is quite apparent. With two, four, and even more Masses on a Sunday morning, pastors with their assistants scarcely have time to distribute even the sacred Hosts to the throngs of the faithful.

Chapter 7

With Dyed Garments

IT IS an indisputable article of Faith, that in order to be cleansed from sin, original or actual, we need the application of the Precious Blood of Jesus Christ, in which alone we are justified and freed from the anger of God. "Almost all things, according to the law, are cleansed with blood: and without shedding of blood there is no remission." (*Heb.* 9:22). "Christ died for us; much more therefore, being now justified by his blood, shall we be saved from wrath through him." (*Rom.* 5:9).

Although the merits of the Precious Blood have been applied to our souls in the holy sacrament of Baptism, by which we were washed from the stain of original sin in the lustral water which derives its efficacy solely from the Blood of Christ, still our inordinate concupiscences and evil inclinations remain for us. It is necessary, therefore, for us to have recourse to the laver of Christ's Precious Blood again and again, to be cleansed from our actual sins and our daily faults, and to be healed more and more from the effects of sin and from dangerous attachments and baneful tendencies. Hence St. Fulgentius, one of the Fathers of the Church, says that the application of the Precious Blood to every Christian is indispensable, from the time of his birth to old age—that is, until death.

Another undeniable truth that shows forth the necessity of applying the Precious Blood to our souls, is the doctrine that nothing defiled can enter the Kingdom of Heaven. Since the fall of Adam, man is a vessel of defilement and must be washed in the Blood of the Lamb before the gates of Heaven will be opened to him. No one will become a citizen of the abode of the elect unless he be marked by the Blood of Christ. "Blessed are they that wash their robes in the blood of the lamb; that they may have a right to the tree of life, and may enter in by the gates into the city." (*Apoc.* 22:14). The Abbot Rupert expresses this doctrine of the Apostle in these words: "Nobody will see God unless He is sprinkled with the Blood of Christ."

For this reason Our Lord has left us in His Church many means by which His Precious Blood is applied to our souls. The Holy Eucharist is, as a sacrifice and as a sacrament, the heart of the activity of the Precious Blood, but the other sacraments are the vessels, the veins through which this life-giving stream of grace is conducted from the Heart of Jesus into the souls of men for their sanctification. The sacraments are a continuation of the earthly life of our Divine High-priest. They are wonderful inventions and dispensations of His divine love and mercy, disclosing the supernatural in natural forms, as they are visible signs of the invisible graces of the Precious Blood. "In that day there shall be a fountain open to the house of David, and to the inhabitants of Jerusalem, for the washing of the sinner." (*Zach.* 13:1).

What would happen to us without the constant activity of the Precious Blood in the Church? The tyranny of sin would become intolerable; there would be no striving after "the things that are above," and we should relapse into the worst forms of heathenism. But the Precious Blood exercises a constant warfare against evil and raises a mighty bulwark against the inroads of sin. It is to us a source of light and warmth and strength in our daily trials and combats. In death, when all other lights go out, the Precious Blood offers to the anxious soul its only light and hope and courage.

The Blood of Christ shed and renewed daily for sins! Do we realize the enormous iniquity of sin, with which men sport and jest and which many drink like water? O terrible necessity of the Blood of Jesus, which alone is efficacious in wiping out sin! Sin frustrates the designs of God and destroys as much as it can, the merits of our Redeemer's Blood. The sinner sees the Blood of his Saviour flowing from His Sacred Wounds and yet by his sins he helps to widen and deepen those wounds. But what could inspire the penitent sinner with more confidence in God than a deep devotion to the Precious Blood? Who could lose faith in Jesus when he sees Him bleeding for us? "My daughter," writes St. Jane Frances de Chantal, "often considers how it is said in the Gospel that Jesus Christ loved us, and washed us in His Blood, and observe that He did not wait to love us until we were washed from our impurities; but He loved us when we were vile and impure creatures, and then washed us."

The Sacred Body of our Redeemer covered with Blood is an eloquent and irresistible proof that God does not wish to condemn us, but promises that we shall be saved for all eternity, if only we accept His proffered graces. The prophet Micheas foretells the deluge of the Precious Blood when he writes: "He will cast all our sins into the bottom of the sea." (*Mich.* 7:19). Every drop of this Blood is a voice that proclaims: "God doth not want the death of a sinner but that he be converted and live." In a vision St. Mechtilde saw and heard our Divine Saviour Himself encourage despondent sinners to have recourse to His Precious Blood.

In the holy Sacrament of Penance Jesus Christ has prepared for us a laver of His own Blood, to which we have free access in order to cleanse our souls from every defilement. Isaias said: "Wash yourselves, be clean," (*Is.* 1:16), and the Church invites us in these words taken from her divine office:

> *Venite, quotquot criminum*
> *Funesta labes inficit;*
> *In hoc salutis balneo,*
> *Qui se lavat, mundabitur.*

> Come, bathe you in that healing flood,
> All ye who mourn with sin opprest;
> Your only hope is Jesus' Blood,
> His Sacred Heart your only rest.

The Precious Blood of Jesus, the Blood of His sorrowful, suffering, agonizing Heart at Gethsemani, will help us to excite in our hearts acts of lively contrition. All sins, as our Lord Himself says, originate in the heart; therefore He wanted to expiate our crimes in His Heart first, before He carried them in His Body to the Cross on Calvary. As the grape in the wine press yields its juice to the heavy weight placed upon it, so the Blood of Jesus flowed from His Sacred Heart under the weight of sin and the intense agony of His soul. From this precious grape of the Sacred Heart the purple wine of salvation was pressed. "I have trodden the wine press alone." (*Is.* 63:3).

Since from the heart proceeds all evil and since the heart is the battleground of our spiritual combats, the remedy must be applied to the heart. The first and essential part of penance, therefore, must be the penance of the heart, or contrition. The heart must be detached from all bonds that connect it with sin and bad habits. "A sacrifice to God is an afflicted spirit: a contrite and humbled heart, O God, thou wilt not despise."

Come, then, all you children of Adam driven out of the Garden of Eden and behold your Saviour in the Garden of Olives! My God, where art Thou? I beheld Thee prostrate on the ground, Thy sacred countenance in the dust, Thy body weeping tears of Blood from every pore, expiating my sins and paving the way to the Garden of Paradise that I might reign with Thee there forever! In preparing for confession if you feel that your act of contrition is not whole-hearted, think of Our Lord in Gethsemani, and the bleeding, agonizing Heart of Jesus will supply what is wanting in your sorrow for sin, if only you have a good will and a sincere desire for a hearty contrition.

But "you have not yet resisted unto blood, striving against sin," as St. Paul admonishes us. (*Heb.* 12:4). A true detestation of sin must be accompanied by a firm purpose of amendment. As contrition is the penance of the heart, so a good resolution is the penance of the will. It is certainly not from a want of sufficient knowledge, nor out of malice, that we so easily into our bad habits, but from the weakness of a will enervated by sensuality. The Blood of the Atonement is the powerful antidote to the allurements of pleasure, and devotion to this Blood cannot fail to strengthen the will against the seductions of sin. The Blood of Christ is honored and glorified by the fruits of a good will in the Sacrament of Penance, because in this sacrament it can unfold and display its purifying power and sanctifying activity. "Blessed be the God and Father of our Lord Jesus Christ, who hath predestinated us unto the adoption of children through Jesus Christ unto himself: according to the purpose of his will: unto the praise of the glory of his grace, in which he hath graced us in his beloved Son, in whom we have redemption through his blood, the remission of sins, according to the riches of his grace." (*Eph.* 1:3-7).

By a contrite confession of our sins, followed by the absolution of the priest, we cause the Blood of Jesus to flow from His Sacred Heart into our souls for their purification and sanctification. In sacramental absolution that yearning of the Royal Penitent for the cleansing effect of the Precious Blood is fulfilled: "Thou shalt sprinkle me with hyssop, and I shall be cleansed; thou shalt wash me, and I shall be made whiter than snow." When the priest raises his hand to absolve the penitent sinner, he sprinkles him, so to speak, with the Blood of Christ. "Making peace through the blood of his cross, both as to the things that are on earth, and the things that are in heaven." (*Col.* 1:20). St. Magdalen de Pazzi once saw, in a heavenly vision, a fiery stream of the Blood of our Redemption poured out over the soul of one of the nuns in her convent the moment the priest pronounced absolution over her, and this Blood imparted to her fellow-sister such enchanting beauty that the saint could not but exclaim with joy: "Let this stream flow also over me, O Lord!"

The Precious Blood of Jesus which is poured over the sinner in confession imparts to the humble and contrite soul an indescribable beauty, and fills it with such courage and strength that it is enabled to resist temptations and preserve its nobility and royal beauty. What is the beauty of the human soul? Behold a dead body— how hideous, how gruesome it is! It does not see, it does not hear, it does not feel, it moves neither hand nor foot. The forehead is cold as marble, the mouth overflows with nauseating matter; the lips are black and the whole body emits pestilential odors which fill those who approach it with loathing and drive them away in horror. What makes the dead body so hideous? The soul has fled. This is a picture of the soul in mortal sin when the Holy Ghost withdraws from it. Now, if the body owes its charm and beauty to its vivifying principle, to the soul in its natural state, what splendor and glory must this same soul possess in its supernatural state of sanctifying grace? The sun is so beautiful, so brilliant, that its departing rays, shining upon the broken windows of an old dilapidated house in the distance, convert even that shack into a palace of shimmering gold. But St. Bonaventure assures us that if God should destine the soul in habitual grace [i.e., Sanctifying Grace], instead of the sun, to illuminate the world, it would diffuse more light and splendor than the sun. The reason for all this is that, in the state of grace, the soul is the temple of the Holy Ghost; God dwells in it and communicates to it as much of His own glory as the creature can bear, and thus, in a measure—as St. Thomas teaches—deifies it. Now, Sanctifying Grace, the highest gift of the soul, is the fruit of the Precious Blood and a reflection of its beauty.

Sacramental confession and absolution may also be called the formal and expressed renewal of the holy covenant made between God and the penitent soul and signed by the Blood of Christ, as foreshadowed in the testament between God and the people of Israel. "If we confess our sins, he is faithful and just to forgive us our sins." (*1 Jn.* 1:9) ". . . and the blood of Jesus Christ his Son cleanseth us from all sin." (*1 Jn.* 1:7). Every worthy confession is a realization of the words of consecration at Mass: "For this is the Chalice of My Blood, of the new and eternal testament: the mystery of faith: which shall be shed for you and for many unto the remission of sins."

All satisfaction intended as an expiation for sin and as a reparation to the outraged justice and majesty of God, has its satisfactory value from the Blood of the Atonement. This divine Blood liberates us from the slavery of our bad habits, ransoms us from the thraldom of Satan, and makes us children of God and heirs of Heaven. "God the Father hath delivered us from the power of darkness, and hath translated us into the Kingdom of the Son of his love, in whom we have redemption, through the blood of his cross." In this holy Sacrament of Penance, says St. Bonaventure, that feeling of sadness and depression caused by sin is driven out of the soul by the Blood of the Redeemer, which is a purveyor of heavenly peace and happiness. *"Sanguis Christi sanat poenam tristitiæ corda fidelium consolando."*

Chapter 8

Plentiful Redemption

NO ONE likes to be burdened with debts. He who does not care to pay his bills is considered an undesirable member of the community. After meeting all his just obligations squarely, every man is desirous of bettering his condition in life, is bent on acquiring a home and laying aside a competency for the future. This is the rule of everyday life. "The children of this world are wiser in their generation than the children of light."

Coming from the confessional, where the guilt of sin has been taken from you and the eternal punishment forgiven, and feeling that peace and happiness which the world cannot give, has it ever occurred to you that you are still in debt? Unless the penitent elicits an act of contrition sincere and intense enough to equal the malice of his sin, the obligation of satisfying divine justice by some temporal punishment, to be undergone in this life or in the next, generally remains. The small penance imposed and faithfully performed is usually not sufficient to discharge this debt, which goes on increasing from confession to confession, from year to year.

Adam obtained forgiveness for his sin, but what punishment did it not entail upon himself and his posterity, even after he had confessed to God and expiated it by tears of real contrition! Moses, who received the Ten Commandments from God and was so zealous in inculcating their observance, whose holiness shone from his countenance and struck terror into the hearts of the Israelites, was refused entrance into the promised land because of his mistrust in God. At the very time David was assured of pardon for his sin, he was also reminded that he would yet have to endure a heavy punishment for that sin.

The penitential discipline, or the ancient practice of canonical penance in the Church, imitating the example of St. Paul, is ample proof of the truth which St. Augustine expresses in these words: "Thou leavest not unchastised, O Lord, the sins of even those whom Thou hast pardoned." The very admission to canonical penance in the early Church was considered already a great benefit. "Sin," wrote St. Ambrose to the Emperor Theodosius the Great, after the massacre of Thessalonica, "is effaced only by tears; no angel, no archangel can remit it on any other condition. The Lord Himself forgives only those who do penance. I advise, entreat, warn thee to submit to it."

The Church continues to proclaim her penitential seasons and to insist upon the necessity of practicing penance according to the words of Christ: "Unless you do penance, you shall all likewise perish." In one of her apparitions to Bernadette at Lourdes, the Blessed Virgin Mary, the Mother of Mercy, looking over the world with an expression of intense sadness, exclaimed: "Penance, penance, penance!" How our weak human nature shrinks from the mere mention of penance! But our holy Mother the Church is ever at our side with her consoling doctrines of mercy and pardon.

"An indulgence is the remission of a debt contracted towards both God and the Church, to which the sinner is liable even after having received the pardon of his sins. This remission is made in virtue and by means of the application of the superabundant merits of Christ and His saints, by the authority of the lawful pastors, who grant it for a just and reasonable motive. Hence we conclude, that an indulgence is at the same time a payment, solutio, and a remission, absolutio. It is a rigorous payment of the debt contracted by the sinner, for the whole penalty is exacted to the last farthing; it is a remission, because the sum paid does not come from the sinner's own funds, he being destitute of any, but from the inexhaustible treasure of the Church.

"Indulgences are granted, and to a certain extent reckoned, according to the rules of ancient canonical penances, or canons, which counted by days, by periods of forty days (Quarantines), and by years. But it would be inaccurate to assert that indulgences are nothing but the remission of canonical penances that would have been imposed on the sinner according to ancient discipline; for, as St. Thomas observes, such a doctrine expressly derogates from the privilege granted by Christ to St. Peter in the words. 'whatsoever thou shalt loose on earth it shall be loosed also in heaven.' (*Matt.* 16:19).

"Indulgences have in the eyes of God the exact value set forth in the granting of them by the Church. 'I will give to thee the keys of the kingdom of heaven;' but temporal punishments due to sins forgiven exclude from the kingdom of heaven; hence, the Church has the power to remit temporal punishments; in other words, to grant indulgences, and we may rest assured that the indulgence is accepted by God in that quantity which the Church establishes; otherwise it would be useless to speak, for instance, of indulgences of one hundred or two hundred days as of distinct grants. If the Church has the power to dispose of Christ's Precious Blood in the forgiveness of sin, it is quite fitting that she should be able equally to dispose of its merits for remitting the lesser debt, the punishment. This is that 'plentiful redemption' of which the Psalmist sings. Did not our Lord grant to the penitent thief on the cross this bountiful redemption when He said: 'This day thou shalt be with me in paradise?' St. Paul also grants to a sinner who has given sufficiently strong proof of repentance a solemn remission of the penance imposed upon him. (*2 Cor.* 2:10-11).

"From all this it is clear, that an indulgence does not mean a pardon of sin; it rather supposes, on the contrary, that sin has been forgiven in the sacrament of confession. Much less does it mean a 'license to commit sin.' These are monstrous notions of Protestants and need not be refuted here. To gain a plenary indulgence it is necessary,   1) to be in a state of grace;   2) to have no attachment to venial sin;   3) faithfully to perform certain appointed works. An indulgence does not even deliver the sinner, though repentant and even pardoned, from the consequences implied in the very idea of a sincere repentance; e.g., from the obligation of restoring stolen goods, or retracting calumnies, or avoiding occasions of relapse. It is difficult to understand how Protestants can profess to reject the Catholic conception of indulgences, and yet believe, as most of them do, that after death there will be a 'general indulgence,' when all sins will be forgiven both as to guilt and penalty."

The explanations of Lepicier on Indulgences are so luminous and satisfactory that we cannot refrain from quoting this eminent divine at length in this article, which we consider important on account of the many indulgences to be gained in the Archconfraternity of the Precious Blood, and on account of the general indifference towards indulgences among the faithful. "We pass over indulgences," says the Curé of Ars, "as we walk over a cornfield after the harvest. At the end of our lives we shall rue this very much."

By gaining indulgences, we appreciate properly the Price of our Redemption. "You have been bought with a great price." Indulgences apply the merits of the Precious Blood to our souls. They are sentences of mercy and pardon from the "Lamb of God Who taketh away the sins of the world." As long as we are not free from temporal punishments due to sin, we cannot enjoy the beatific vision in Heaven. If we die with this debt, although in the state of grace, God will have to cast from Himself into the flames of Purgatory. Therefore, if we truly love God with our whole heart we will strive to remove everything already in this world that may stand between us and our Lord, so that He can press us at once to His loving heart without being obliged to send us into a painful exile. With this unpaid debt against us we fell as if our Lord should say to us, touch me not until you have risen completely from the grave of sin and glorified yourself with my Precious Blood by the use of indulgences or penances.

"To become a saint it is sufficient to gain all the indulgences possible."—St. Alphonsus de Liguori. "Indulgences are such excellent things that I feel unable to praise and exalt their value sufficiently. The only thing left for me to do is to beg and exhort you all, by the love and respect you owe to God, to esteem them highly, and to seek to profit by them with all possible care."—St. Ignatius de Loyola. Our Divine Lord told St. Bridget, "Go to Rome: there the streets are golden paved and bedewed with the blood of martyrs; there, because of the Indulgences their merits have won, the road to Heaven is shortened."

Bearing in mind that indulgences are a means by which the Precious Blood of Christ wipes out our debt of temporal punishment and remembering that there is perhaps no Confraternity in the Church that offers us a larger appropriation of satisfactory merits and few richer in indulgences than the Archconfraternity of the Precious Blood, the members of this Archconfraternity will be alert every Sunday in looking over their leaflet or their Manual for the indulgences to be gained during the week, just as a businessman is quick to look up the market quotations every morning in his daily paper for temporal gains.

Chapter 9

Reparation

TO UNDERSTAND the need and importance of Reparation one must first realize the enormity and evil consequences of sin, and the base ingratitude which it involves toward Jesus, "Who bought us with a great price." There is nothing that will more readily imbue us with the spirit of Reparation and more surely quicken in us the desire to practice it, than the devout contemplation of Jesus covered with His own Blood and pleading for us to His Heavenly Father. Millions of hardened hearts, which had gone astray like the prodigal son, have been softened into repentance by the bloody wounds in Our Saviour's body. The saints imbibed their hatred of sin and their burning love of God from the flowering wells beneath the Cross.

"But now in Christ Jesus, you who some time were afar off, are made nigh by the blood of Christ." (*Eph.* 2:13). The oblation of this life-giving Blood brings the heathen nigh to the laver of baptism; it arouses in the sinner a sense of guilt and responsibility; and it begets in the devout soul a spirit of Reparation. The voice and the power of the Blood of the God-Man are strikingly portrayed in Holy Writ.

When Abel lay bleeding on the open field, the enormity of sin became suddenly manifest in all its hideousness. It was the first death. Abel had paid the first wages of sin. "And the Lord said to Cain: 'What hast thou done? The voice of thy brother's blood crieth to me from the earth.'" (*Gen.* 4:10). Listen to St. Paul as he opposes the Blood of the Son of God appealing for mercy, to that of the son of Adam crying for vengeance: "But you are come to Jesus, the Mediator of the new testament, and to the sprinkling of blood which speaketh better than that of Abel."

Joseph had been sold into Egypt. Reuben, one of his brethren, knew full well that they could not dare to appear in the sight of their father Jacob without his favorite son Joseph. "And they took his coat, dipped it in the blood of a kid which they had killed, and to the father they said, 'See whether it be thy son's coat or not.'" Jesus, the Lamb, was slain that we might dip our garments in His Blood flowing in the Sacraments, and thus be made worthy to be presented to God the Father, who might well say: A wild beast has indeed torn My child, sin has left its scar on My image and likeness, but it is covered with the purple robe of My Son in whom I am well pleased.

Judas seemed to realize the malice of his sin to a greater degree when he remembered this Blood of love and mercy, as he cried out: "I have sinned in betraying innocent blood." Pilate felt his guilt deeply, and quailed before this Blood of the Atonement, saying: "I am innocent of the blood of this just man." But the wild mob before Pilate's court shouted with hatred toward the Blood of Christ, the power of which they seemed to feel with crushing effect, when they exclaimed: "His blood be upon us and our children." By this expression the Jewish race rejected the Blood of the New Testament, for which all antiquity had sighed through the voices of the Prophets.

By our devotion to the Precious Blood we step into

the breach and proclaim ourselves true followers of
Jesus Christ. When a current of air of high pressure
meets one of low pressure, rain is produced; when the
wave of Jewish hatred met the impulse of Our Lord's
love on the Cross, the fountains of mercy opened and
poured forth the Blood of our Redemption.

The Precious Blood of Jesus was trampled under
foot all during the Passion, by Jew and Gentile, and
should not we, Christ's dearly bought children, be eager
to offer reparation for the horrible desecration of the
Price of our Redemption? Let us, then, in a spirit of
love and devotion, raise a counter-cry to that of the
Jewish people and say with profound veneration: "His
Blood be upon us and upon our children, but in grace
and benediction."

There is not one of us who could not say with St.
Paul: "He has loved me and has given Himself over
for me." Hence there is no one who has not a special
reason to venerate the Precious Blood, and to make
some atonement for his coldness and indifference
towards this gift, more precious than all the treasures
of the world. "Knowing that you were not redeemed
with corruptible things as gold and silver, but with the
precious blood of Christ, as of a lamb unspotted and
undefiled." (*1 Ptr.* 1:18-19).

Holy Mass is the great sacrifice of the New Testament, the most holy, the most sublime, the most powerful means of reparation, because it is the extension
and continuation of the Sacrifice of Calvary, the only
reparation worthy of the infinite majesty of God.

Even in our own day Our Lord is continually pleading with saintly souls to become victims of His love,
victims of reparation. Reparation is one of the chief
characteristics of the devotion to the Sacred Heart;
and it must be one of the principal objects of the devotion to the Precious Blood. "I have given it to you that

you may make atonement with it upon the altar for your souls, and the blood may be for an expiation of the soul." (*Lev.* 17:11).

"Jesus Christ is the Divine Head of His Mystical Body, the Church; and still in a way He prolongs and perpetuates His Personal existence in every one of His members under some one of the characteristic traits of His life on earth. In the ordinary Christian, He continues His private, or as we may say, *His domestic life* at Nazareth. In the Priest, He continues His public career of preaching, and His peculiar *sacrificial office.* In the Religious, He continues His life and office as *Victim.* God also frequently makes choice of *special victims,* gathered from amongst all ranks of Christian society. He communicates to them, for the salvation of their brethren, a large share in the sufferings of His Divine Son, and in the title and office of *Victim* borne by that Son."

Such victims contract a more perfect resemblance to Jesus Crucified, and a more intimate union with Him who desires that they should participate in a larger measure in His sufferings and merits for themselves and for others, as prolific branches of the true Vine. In this sense they may say in the words of St. Paul: "I fill up in my flesh those things that are wanting of the sufferings of Christ." (*Col.* 1:24).

Love is a flame that requires a victim. The flames leaping from the Heart of Jesus are seeking hearts. "My child, give me thy heart." "I am come to cast fire on the earth: and what will I but that it be kindled. And I have a baptism wherewith I am to be baptized: and how am I straightened until it be accomplished?" (*Luke* 12:49). His pent-up love yearns for the opening of His Heart, that the oil of His Sacred Blood may overflow the earth, and spread the fire of His love.

With what tender love and affection Jesus in the

Blessed Sacrament contemplates a soul kneeling in His presence, bowed down with grief at the thought of the coldness and indifference of souls toward their "Spouse of Blood," and with a burning love exclaims: "O Jesus, Thou art not loved as Thou deservest to be loved!" To such a soul Our Lord will say, as He did to Mary Magdalen, "Much has been forgiven her because she loved much;" and it may be added, much will be given her because she loves much. During the Holy Hour, let us strive to excite within ourselves such acts of love and gratitude as may lead us on to a complete immolation of self, so that our hearts with all their affections may be as holocausts of love in the sight of the Prisoner of Love. The essence of Reparation lies in love and suffering. He who does not crave to suffer for the love of Jesus, has not begun to love Him ardently.

At the Crucifixion some wagged their heads and mocked Our Lord; the great throng was idly interested; some passed on silently; and the centurion struck his breast saying: "Truly this was the Son of God." But behold the Sorrowful Mother, St. John, Mary Magdalen and the weeping women beneath the cross in unspeakable anguish because of their love.

Where do we stand? What attitude do we assume toward our dying Saviour? What sentiments do we entertain for Him? To what degree do we share the feelings of our dolorous Mother? How do we express our love and sympathy?

In spirit, let us join the Procession of the Precious Blood to Calvary. Let us, with Simon of Cyrene, bear the precious burden of the Cross, and follow in the blood-stained footprints of the Saviour; and, like Veronica, let us wipe away the Blood from the disfigured countenance of Him who was 'most beautiful among the sons of men,' while we supplicate Him to impress upon our minds the memory of His Sacred Passion, and imprint upon our hearts, as on the veil of Veronica, the ineffaceable traces of His Holy Suffering Face. With the weeping women of Jerusalem, let us kneel before Him who uttered a word of comfort for their sorrow, though His own Heart was breaking. On the heights of Calvary we must fall prostrate beside grief-stricken Magdalen, and mingle the tears of a pardoned sinner with the life-giving stream issuing from the transfixed feet of the Redeemer. In spirit, let us mount the cross of the penitent thief, and cry out with love and confidence to our crucified King—making reparation for those who blaspheme Him, and begging Him for a place in His Kingdom, that we may be near Him forever! Let us draw closer, and stand in the shadow of the Cross beside the disciple whom Jesus loves, and gaze with John into the dying Master's face, and listen to the tender accents of His last bequest: "Son, behold thy Mother." Let us approach that Mother, the Mother of Sorrows, that, by her side, and in union with her, we may offer the Blood of Jesus to the heavenly Father, for ourselves and for all the world. As the centurion, with bowed head, strikes his breast, in presence of the Saviour's opened side, let us strike our breasts, giving in exchange for that Divine Heart, our own sin-stained human hearts, and at the foot of that altar of the Divine Sacrifice, let us offer in oblation our whole selves, in life and in death, while the last drops of the Price of our Redemption are flowing from the pierced Heart of the Saviour of the world.

"As the Divine Bridegroom is 'white and ruddy' (*candidus et rubicundus*—*Cant.* 5:10), His spouse, the human soul, should also shone resplendent in the delicate white of purity and in the fiery red of divine love, which when blended make up the lovely rose-colored garment of grace. O charming heavenly attire of grace in a soul! Brilliant beauty that adorns and delights the garden of God! Who would not desire this adornment, covet this beauty, this roseate raiment of the soul! Thy soul must shine in the rose-colored garment of purity, love and grace, if thou wouldst be admitted to the heavenly wedding feast. Red also reminds thee of the great accounting day, of the dreadful day of judgment. Behold, the Son of man comes on bright, shining clouds; He comes surrounded by the brilliant heavenly court; He comes with great power and majesty. Like the blood-red radiant sun, He appears in the purple clouds of the eternal heavens, in the purple rays of the holy Cross, in the purple splendor of His radiant wounds. The Cross will shine in the heavens, and will cast frightful blood-red rays on the wicked. On the body of the Judge of the world His sacred wounds will shine as fiery purple and terrify all who have rendered His precious blood fruitless and trampled it under foot."—Gihr.

With a lively faith, O Jesus, I offer Thee Thy Precious Blood for those who ignore Thee.

With deep reverence, O Jesus, I offer Thee Thy Precious Blood for those who blaspheme Thee.

With profound adoration, O Jesus, I offer Thee Thy Precious Blood for those who hate Thee.

With sentiments of compassion I offer Thee Thy Precious Blood for those who trample under foot the Price of their Redemption.

Chapter 10

The Blood Shall Be Unto You For a Sign

W E ALL remember the illustration in Bible History, showing the Israelites marking the doorposts of their houses with blood, while the exterminating angel, with drawn sword, is passing overhead. It was a terrible night in Egypt. The Lord was about to send the tenth plague upon Pharaoh and his people by striking down every firstborn in the land—of both man and beast. But God told Moses that He would spare the Israelites, on the condition that they would take of the blood of the paschal lamb "and put it upon both the side posts and on the upper doorposts of the houses, wherein they shall eat it." "And I will pass through the land of Egypt that night, and will kill every firstborn in the land of Egypt, both man and beast: and against all the gods of Egypt I will execute judgments: I am the Lord. And the blood shall be unto you for a sign in the houses where you shall be: and I shall see the blood, and shall pass over you: and the plague shall not be upon you to destroy you, when I shall strike the land of Egypt." (*Ex.* 12:7-13).

If the blood of an animal as a figure of the Blood of the Lamb of God, had the power to ward off the angel of death from the houses of the children of God, what protection may we not expect from the Blood of Jesus,

66

which is shed for us in the Holy Sacrifice of the Mass, and with which we sprinkle our very lips in Holy Communion! St. John Chrysostom, commenting on this passage of Exodus, says: "If the angel withdrew when he saw the blood of the type, how much more will the enemy take to flight when he sees the lips of the faithful, who are the temples of God, red with the real Blood of Christ?"

Therefore a special veneration of the Precious Blood will merit for us also a special protection against the punishments of sin, against the terrible judgments with which God, from time to time, visits this sinful earth. Blessed Gaspar del Bufalo frequently assured his contemporaries that those who foster devotion to the Precious Blood shall obtain special mercy in times of tribulation.

In 1849 Pope Pius IX was driven from Rome by revolutionists. At the time it seemed doubtful whether the Sovereign Pontiff would ever be permitted to return to the Eternal City; but after the Holy Father had promised to extend the celebration of the Feast of the Precious Blood over the entire world, his return to Rome was unexpectedly effected. Henceforth one of his favorite mottoes was, "Place on thy heart one drop of the Precious Blood—and fear nothing."

The decree issued by Pius IX begins with these words: "We have been redeemed by the Precious Blood of Jesus Christ," and it proceeds to explain that, as the Israelites who sprinkled the doorposts of their houses with the blood of the paschal lamb, were spared by the avenging angel, so they can protect themselves with far greater security against the anger of God, who venerate the Precious Blood of Jesus in a special manner. What a powerful invitation from the saintly Pontiff to join the Archconfraternity of the Precious Blood.

St. Clare is said to have warded off the Saracens

from scaling the walls of her convent by having recourse to the Precious Blood in the following prayer: "We beseech Thee, O Lord, help Thy servants whom Thou hast redeemed with Thy Precious Blood." Through the Prophet Ezechiel, God complained that He had sought in vain for one to stand in the gap before Him in favor of the land that He might not destroy it. Our divine Saviour makes a similar plea for reparation to St. Margaret Mary Alacoque: "My justice is irritated and ready to punish secret sinners by manifest chastisements if they do no penance. I wish to have thee know when My justice will be ready to deal its blows upon those criminal heads. It will be when thou wilt feel the weight of My sanctity upon thee. Thou oughtest then to raise thy heart and hands to Heaven by prayers and good works, to present Me continually to My Father as a victim of love immolated for the sins of the world, and place Me as a rampart between the divine justice and sinners in order to obtain My mercy."

The community of saints to which we all belong creates amongst us a common responsibility, in virtue of which both the good and the evil done by one are in a certain sense imputed to the rest. This is why entire communities sometimes have been saved because they contained just one holy soul, known to God alone, as in the case of Putiphar, whose house received abundant blessings only for the sake of Joseph. How often has not the whole mystic body of Christ had to suffer cruel persecutions through faults committed only by certain perverse members, but for which all were to a certain degree jointly answerable.

The very heathens looked upon their plagues as coming from their gods, who had to be placated by sacrifices. Must God always send His avenging angel visibly among us before we believe in His chastisements? The connection of calamities with the sins of which they are the punishment is not always apparent, but to those who believe in the supernatural much is clear which others cannot see; and even with our limited vision we often discern that temporal afflictions or disasters are the result of sin. Did not Our Lord Himself say to the man languishing thirty-eight years at the pool called Bethsaida, "Behold, thou art made whole: sin no more, lest some worse thing happen to thee."

On the other hand, we must be very reserved when there is question of deciding on the punitive character of a divine visitation in the case of individuals, as well as of entire communities, in order not to expose ourselves to the risk of passing unjust and sinful judgments; for it is a consoling fact, that not all God's visitations are necessarily chastisements in the sense of punishments. "And Jesus passing by, saw a man, who was blind from his birth: And his disciples asked him: Rabbi, who hath sinned, this man, or his parents, that he should be born blind? Jesus answered: neither hath this man sinned, nor his parents; but that the works of God should be made manifest to him." (*John* 9:1-3).

Suffering and persecution have ever been the badge of true Christianity, and the greatest saints were subjected to the greatest trials, to give them an opportunity of becoming more like their Master and of treasuring up for themselves greater merit. A time of severe tribulation is often intended by God as a preparation for extraordinary graces or favors. God always sends trials to the souls that are aiming at perfection and this sometimes during their entire lives. "Consider it certain that a person or a congregation that does not suffer and is applauded by all the world, is near a fall."—St. Vincent de Paul.

How can we better qualify ourselves to fulfill the law of expiatory responsibility than by joining the Archconfraternity of the Precious Blood? Its members the

world over present themselves in answer to the call of
the Lord to appease His wrath, and by their continual oblations of the Precious Blood cause our Saviour
to appear with His radiant Five Wounds of mercy forming a magnificent rainbow of promise.

> "O to be sprinkled from the wells
> Of Christ's own sacred Blood excels
> Earth's best and highest bliss:
> The ministers of wrath divine
> Hurt not the happy hearts that shine
> With those red drops of His!"

While in the Old Dispensation God dealt out to His
people speedy and terrible retribution, now unknown
and unsuspected temporal calamities are daily driven
away like clouds before the wind, by the oblation of
the Precious Blood in the Holy Sacrifice of the Mass.

"Countless blessings daily flow from the altar and
diffuse themselves over the vast expanse of the earth.
In the Mass, as on the Cross, Christ is, moreover, 'the
propitiation for our sins, and not for our sins only, but
for those also of the whole world.' (*1 John* 2:2). If this
'sacrifice for sin' were no longer left us, what else would
remain for the world 'But a certain dreadful expecta-
tion of judgment, and the rage of a fire which shall
consume the adversaries?' (*Heb.* 10:27). Although the
Lord sees that 'great as is the wickedness of men on
the earth, and that all the thought of their heart is
bent upon evil at all times,' yet He no longer says: 'I
will destroy man, whom I have created, from the face
of the earth;' for He promised that no flood should
henceforth come to destroy all flesh, and that He would
no more curse the earth on account of man. (*Gen.* 9:15).
But why? Because the Lord God 'scents the sweet savor'
of the Sacrifice. (*Gen.* 8:21), that is offered daily on
thousands and thousands of altars 'for the salvation

of the world.' Unceasingly does the Holy Sacrifice of the Mass fasten an eternally new bond between Heaven and earth, between God and man. This is the true eternal fire that is never extinguished, the sacrificial fire which burns day and night in the sanctuary in honor of the Almighty."—Gihr.

"Most Precious Blood of Jesus, Our Lord, cry for mercy for us to Thy Divine Father, and deliver us from all evil."

"Spare, O Lord, spare Thy people whom Thou hast redeemed with Thy Precious Blood."

"Eternal Father, sign us with the Blood of the Immaculate Lamb, as Thou didst sign the dwellings of Thy people."

"Being now justified by his blood, shall we be saved from wrath through him." (*Rom.* 5:9).

Chapter 11

Balm For the Sick And Consolation For the Dying

PAIN, as beautifully described by Pére Laurent, not only respects the past, that is, it is not only expiatory in character, but it is one of the finest signs of God's mindfulness for us in the present, as well as for the future. We are afflicted that we may be saved, and the hand that wounds is also the hand that heals. Through suffering, new spiritual life is borne from this partial destruction of our being. God allows jealous rivalries, cruel disappointments, unexpected humiliations, to accomplish this aim; here He shatters a fortune, there He humbles a pride; dissipates this man's dreams for the future, strikes that man in his affections; maybe for another all earthly happiness will be swallowed up at a blow.

In all this lies the mission of pain—to bring God nearer to us and to raise us up to God. It detaches us from this wicked world and our sinful habits. Our sufferings ascend to Heaven like sweet incense, even as a log is raised to the skies by applying fire to it and letting it go up in flame and smoke.

Pain is a grace which sanctifies the soul; through it, a sort of mystic union is effected which unites the life of the suffering soul to the very life of the suffering God-Man, and in this contact of the soul with God, pain is transmuted into power of redemption. Those who are patient and resigned to the will of God, acquire a likeness to their Divine Master, assuming the lineaments of the Crucified, especially if their sufferings be, in a measure, undeserved. They are identified with Jesus Christ, as victims of His special love, offered in expiation for the sins of this wicked world, and as such, they become a part of the vast scheme of atonement.

"Without the shedding of blood there is no remission," says St. Paul. It matters little whether it be the blood of bodily wounds or tears, which are the blood of the soul. "The good God," says the Curé of Ars, "asks not for the martyrdom of our bodies, but for the martyrdom of our hearts and wills." There is an apostolate of suffering, as well as an apostolate of prayer and labor. "For whom he foreknew, he also predestinated to be made conformable to the image of his son." (*Rom.* 8:29). Jesus Christ continues to make reparation through those whose mission it is to suffer with Him for this sin-sick world. This is what St. Paul meant when, persecuted like his Master, he said of himself, "I fill up these things what are wanting of the sufferings of Christ."

What a consoling truth this should be for the sick, especially for nervous persons who feel like outcasts from human society, and frequently consider themselves abandoned even by God. Their past sins, and even their smaller faults, weigh heavily upon them. They imagine that God has forsaken them on account of their mistakes in life, and their offenses against Him, and they feel that neither in this life nor in the next can they receive forgiveness or attain happiness.

Look up to the Cross, despondent souls, you who share in the bitter abandonment of your dying Saviour, and listen to the words of the Beloved Disciple, "He has loved us and washed us in His Blood," and

He loves us now; as much as He did then.

> "Oh sweetest Blood, that can implore
> Pardon of God, and heaven restore,
> The heaven which sin has lost,
> While Abel's blood for vengeance pleads,
> What Jesus shed still intercedes
> For those who wrong Him most."

For neurotic persons, at a certain stage in their despondency, the future has naught in store but gloom and despair. "And I wept much," writes St. John of what he saw as a pilgrim in Heaven, "because no man was found worthy to open the book nor to see it." To this book, by which is meant the history of the fall and redemption of mankind, the future of our own lives may be compared; it is a sealed book to us, and a most perplexing riddle, full of anxieties and fearful uncertainties, especially for the nerve-racked. "And one of the ancients said to me:" continues St. John, "weep not; behold the lion of the tribe of Juda, the root of David, hath prevailed to open the book, and loose the seven seals thereof. And I saw . . . a lamb standing as it were slain . . . and he came and took the book out of the right hand of him that sat on the throne. And when he had opened the book . . . they sung a new canticle, saying: 'Thou art worthy, O Lord, to take the book, and to open the seals thereof; because thou wast slain, and has redeemed us to God, in thy blood, out of every tribe, and tongue, and people, and nation, and hast made us to our God a kingdom and priests, and we shall reign on the earth.'" (*Apoc.* 5:4-10).

Therefore, weep not, dear despondent soul! The Lamb that was slain, but rose again on the third day, as the Lion of the tribe of Juda, will lead you safely through your labyrinth of gloom and despair, if you will but cling to Him by the virtue of hope. The Lamb that was slain becomes the Lion of the tribe of Juda. "Ideo victor quia victima," says St. Augustine, "Christ is the victor because He became a victim."

St. Paul encourages us in these words: "In all things we suffer tribulation, but are not distressed: we are straightened, but are not destitute: we suffer persecution, but are not forsaken: we are cast down, but we perish not. For which cause we faint not: but though our outward man is corrupted, yet the inward man is renewed day by day."

Thus, from this seeming destruction of your being, you will emerge renewed in heart and character, your soul purified and sanctified, and worthy to sing a new canticle of life. "These are they who are come out of great tribulation, and have washed their robes and have made them white in the blood of the Lamb." (*Apoc.* 7:14). "For the Lamb, which is in the midst of the throne, shall rule them and shall lead them to the fountains of the waters of life, and God shall wipe away all tears from their eyes." (*Apoc.* 7:17). In the light of our future glory, our present tribulations should seem light and transient indeed!

We are on our way to life everlasting, to the land of the living, to *the* world, to *the* life, to *the* light. The road thither leads us through long and dark tunnels, then again up steep paths covered with thorns and thistles; our present infirmities will serve but to shorten the way. All Heaven is awaiting us at the other end.

The Blood of Christ is truly a balm for the sick, and a consolation for the dying. The sacrament of Extreme Unction is the channel through when the Precious Blood is conveyed to the sick, during their last moments, by means of the application of the holy oils to the wounds of body and soul.

The devotion to the Blood of Jesus has the wonderful distinction of dispelling the fear of death, and the dread of meeting our Judge. "Having, therefore, a confidence in the entering into the holies by the blood of Christ." (*Heb.* 10:19).

"The Blood of our Lord, wherever it is found, must produce great confidence in God; confidence in God is its primary and principal effect. Not only does it give us confidence through the belief that we have been bought at so great a price, but it gives confidence by a kind of heredity, a psychological transformation in the spirit that receives it. We become spiritually, supernaturally sanguine. We expect everything from God, precisely because we have in our veins that precious blood that makes the heart of the Son of God throb with unlimited confidence in the goodness of the Father."—Vonier.

"The Blood of Jesus Christ," says St. Bernard, "speaks with trumpet tones, not of the judgments of God, but of His mercies." The great St. Thomas Aquinas calls the Precious Blood the key to the heavenly Paradise. How consoling are the words of St. John Chrysostom: "This Blood has the power to drive away the evil spirits and to draw to our side the good angel, aye, the King of angels, and to blazon the way to Heaven." Ah! how well the saints knew the wonderful power of the Blood of the God-Man! "O Blood of Jesus, shed for love of me," exclaimed St. Francis Carraccioli at the hour of death, "Thou belongest to me. I ask it of Thee, O Lord! Thou canst not refuse it to me, because it is mine." Then he devoutly kissed the five wounds of the Crucified and repeated again and again: "Blood of my Jesus, thou art mine and only with Thee and through Thee I hope to be saved."

Thou, too, discouraged soul, art stretched upon a cross of pain, twixt earth and Heaven; being above the earth, its comforts and vain hopes can give thee no relief; and since thou art yet fastened to the earth,

Heaven and its consolations are far from thee. Look up to the Cross of Christ, despondent soul—nay, happy soul, that sharest the bitter abandonment of thy dying Saviour. For thy sake, His cry of agony, "My God, my God! why hast thou forsaken me?" is piercing the very heavens. Courage, sad heart, thy God has not forsaken thee. The Beloved Disciple says: "And I heart a loud voice in Heaven saying: 'Now is come salvation and strength, and the kingdom of our God, and the power of his Christ; because the accuser of our brethren is cast forth, who accused them before our God day and night. And they overcame him by the blood of the Lamb,'" (*Apoc.* 12:10-11).

You, who sometime were afar off, were made nigh by the Blood of Christ in the sacrament of Baptism. Your soul, stained by sin, was time and again washed by the sacrament of Penance. In Holy Communion you were brought still nearer to Jesus. You entered into the closest relationship with Our Lord so that His divine life pulsated in yours. In Confirmation your soul received the impression of an indelible seal which marked you as the property of God. In how many Masses was your soul sprinkled with the Precious Blood of your Redeemer! And now in the sacrament of Extreme Unction and in the plenary indulgence for the hour of death the Precious Blood achieves its final triumph here on earth so that you may appear with the robe of royalty before your Judge.

In the words of the Dies Irae you may well exclaim:

> Faint and weary thou has sought me,
> On the Cross of suffering bought me;
> Shall such grace in vain be brought me?
>
> Thou Who didst the robber hear,
> Biddest me with hope draw near.

Yes, bid me come to Thee above,
With Thy saints to sing Thy love.

Now you are prepared to join the saints, now you are entitled to sing; and the echo from your death-chamber will be: With Thy saints to sin Thy love. From Heaven the words of St. John fall like a gentle dew upon your grave: "Blessed are they that wash their robes in the Blood of the Lamb!"

Chapter 12

Redemption For the Souls In Purgatory

HEAVEN is an immediate reward for perfection already attained. "There shall not enter into it anything defiled." (*Apoc.* 21; 27). A soul, therefore, with the slightest imperfection in Heaven would be an object of horror to itself and to others. We often hear people say that if this or that person is admitted to Heaven they do not want to go there. Even we, who are fully aware of our own faults, would be unwilling to put up in Heaven with the imperfections of others. With how much greater right must not God, who created Heaven for the perfect enjoyment of the elect, demand that we be perfect before we enter Heaven. "Be ye perfect even as your Father which is in Heaven is perfect." Which is more unlike a Christian and harder to believe, that all those persons whom we dislike or with whom we would not associate, will go to Hell to suffer eternally, or that they will go to a place of purification to suffer for a time, and then be associated with the blessed for all eternity.

Again, we are enjoined not only to be perfect, but "Thou shalt love the Lord thy God with thy whole heart, and with thy whole soul, and with thy whole mind." This is a commandment, and we cannot enter Heaven until we have fulfilled this commandment. But how few there are who, at the hour of death, can say they have thus loved God? Is not rather the sentiment, this world is good enough for me, commonly entertained and often expressed? How few really hunger after justice and seek the things that are above and therefore deserve the title of blessed? Freed from all earthly attachments, which it now realizes did not fully satisfy it, the soul in Purgatory yearns with an intense longing for the presence of its Maker and Redeemer and with a love of God which, in the words of St. Francis de Sales, "gives birth to cruel sufferings."

Purgatory is a place of banishment and suffering. As such it is characterized by Our Lord, who calls it a prison: "Thou shalt not go out from thence till thou repay the last farthing." (*Matt.* 5:26). St. Paul describes the state of that prison in the words: "But he himself shall be saved, yet so as by fire." (*1 Cor.* 3:15). The sufferings of the Holy Souls, however, are not unmixed with peace and inward happiness.

"I do not think," says St. Catherine of Genoa in her treatise on Purgatory, "that any joy can be found to be compared with that of the souls of Purgatory, unless it be that of the saints in Paradise. And this joy is augmented every day, thanks to the influence of God on these souls, which constantly increases in proportion as the hindrance to its action on them diminishes . . . At the same time, they suffer such exceeding pain, that no tongue can describe it, and no intellect could understand it in the smallest degree, if God did not make it known by a special favor. In short, the souls in Purgatory unite two things which seem to us irreconcilable: they experience an extreme joy and at the same time suffer severe torments, without one neutralizing the other."

A similar relation of mystic pain and joy may be found in the lives of the saints here on earth. After her heart had been pierced with a dart of love by an angel, St. Teresa says: "The pain thereof was so intense, that it forced deep groans from me; but the sweetness which this extreme pain caused in me was so excessive, that there was no desiring to be free from it; nor is the soul then content with anything less than God. This is not a corporal but a *spiritual* pain, though the body does not fail to participate a little in it, yea, a great deal. I could not understand how it was possible that pain and joy could be united; that corporal pain and spiritual joy were compatible, I knew very well; but that so excessive a spiritual pain should be compatible with so extraordinary a spiritual joy, did quite astonish me."

"Poor Souls, indeed," exclaims St. Leonard of Port Maurice, "whose earthly banishment is at an end, but forbidden to enter the promised land. They have claim to heavenly riches, but suffer extreme destitution. They are kings and queens every one, but in bondage. Glorious victors all, but yet uncrowned. Companions of the angels and citizens of Heaven, yet in the bowels of the earth. God is their spouse, but as yet their judge, who 'delivered them to the torturers.'"

While the stains of sin with which these souls sullied their baptismal robe here on earth are all cleansed the moment they enter the next world, so that they are at once constituted in perfect holiness and are therefore called Holy Souls, they are nevertheless retained in the purifying flames of Purgatory to discharge the debt of punishment contracted by sins indeed forgiven, but not entirely expiated during life. They are there to acquit themselves of an obligation. Hence our Lord speaks of "paying the last farthing."

These prisoners are powerless in the purifying flames of Purgatory; but what copious means we have at our disposal to help them by reason of the communion of saints according to the doctrine of vicarious satisfaction as expressed by good works, indulgences and above all by the oblation of the Holy Sacrifice of the Mass. The sacrificial Blood of the Mass offered in behalf of the suffering souls will cancel the penalty for which they are held captives more readily than the fires of Purgatory.

The mercy of God manifests itself by multiplying the means of pardon and the opportunities for help. Thus the Church has endowed the Confraternity of the Precious Blood with extraordinary indulgences, and all these indulgences are applicable to the suffering souls of Purgatory, so that its members can, by merely making the intention, convert it into one of the richest confraternities for the Poor Souls. By so doing, we apply all the satisfactory merits of these indulgences and good works to these needy souls, while the meritorious value of such charitable acts is inalienable and always remains ours as a reward in Heaven. "In Jesus Christ we lose nothing by helping others, grace increases in proportion as we give and the crock of oil emptied by charity into the vessels brought to her filling, overflows the more for what it pours out."—Peter of Blois. We liberate God's dearest children from prison and make them our advocates in Heaven, where they will succor us in our temporal and spiritual needs. Giving alms to the Poor Souls is an act of mercy that will obtain for us mercy and insure for us a hundredfold reward and our own speedy deliverance from Purgatory. How beautiful is this doctrine of the Communion of Saints!

There is no one so helpless, so desirous of the Precious Blood, as the suffering souls in Purgatory; and there is no means at our disposal so efficacious in helping these souls as the Precious Blood. It is related of Blessed Henry Suso, that he entered into a compact with another member of the Dominican order, that the one who survived the other should say a Mass in honor of the Passion of our Lord every Friday and offer a Mass for the departed every Monday during an entire year. Hearing of the death of his friend, Henry did not fail to offer many prayers and good works for the repose of his soul, but neglected to say the Masses stipulated in the agreement. One day the deceased appeared to him and complained bitterly of his unfaithfulness to his promise. Henry replied that he never omitted to recommend his soul to God. "But the Sacred Blood of Jesus is wanting," said the departed, "where are the Masses that affords us so much relief?" By fulfilling his promise, Blessed Henry soon had the happiness of seeing his friend released from Purgatory.

Ah! how keenly these suffering souls now realize the immense value of this Divine Blood! With what fervor they would offer it in expiation for their sins, if the time to do so were not past! Like holy mendicants, they surround those who are wont to offer the Precious Blood for them, at the Holy Sacrifice of the Mass. They see this holy well overflowing on our altars into thousands of souls, "In that day there shall be a fountain open to the house of David, and to the inhabitants of Jerusalem." (*Zach.* 13:1); but, like the poor man at the pool of Bethsaida, they must wait for some angel to move the waters of this sacred pool in their behalf.

The angels ever adoring the Blessed Sacrament are willing, and do but await our bidding, to be the ministers of our mercy; for this adorable Blood is ours—ours to receive, ours to dispose of. The Archangel Michael is mentioned in the Office and Mass of the Church as the guardian of the souls of the just. "Michael, my Archangel, I have established thee prince over all souls that are to be received into My Kingdom."

It is estimated that there are at present about 300,000 Masses said daily, and at every Mass there are angels present. Let us invite these angels the world over to take the 300,000 chalices with the Sacred Blood from the altar and bring them to St. Michael, the guardian of Purgatory, that he may present this priceless argosy to the Heavenly Father for the relief and release of the suffering souls. We can all do this at Mass and thereby cause joy to the divine Victim whose Heart's Blood is filling Purgatory with consolation, and we ourselves will take a new interest in the Mass and a delight in this simple way of honoring the Precious Blood and doing a great work of mercy.

Think of this grand procession of angels with the Holy Grail hastening at your command from earth to Purgatory to succor the Poor Souls, while Our Redeemer is offering Himself on 300,000 altars; of the acclamations of delight when this tide of Divine Blood reaches the flames of the truly banished children of Eve; and—after this flood of redemption has done its work—of the glorious array of purified souls leaving the land of woe and, in company with their guardian angels, flying to the realms of eternal bliss!

If, in the language of Our Saviour, you should "make unto you friends of the mammon of iniquity, that when you shall fail they may receive you into everlasting dwellings," how much the more should you employ the precious gold of Christ's Divine Blood, in making for yourselves, special and everlasting friends in Heaven by offering continual oblations of the Blood of Jesus, in behalf of the Souls in Purgatory!

St. Magdalen de Pazzi was wont to offer it fifty times a day for the suffering souls, and it was revealed to her how great was the number she thus liberated. Following her example, let us often say: "O Eternal Father, I offer Thee through the hands of the Sorrowful Mother, the Precious Blood of They Son for the suffering souls in Purgatory."

Oh, how anxious the holy souls must be to see this devotion propagated! Therefore, while we are zealous in promoting the devotion to the Precious Blood here on earth, let us be still more so in releasing members from Purgatory to adore this Divine Blood of our Redeemer in Heaven. "Thou also by the blood of thy testament hast sent forth thy prisoners out of the pit, wherein is no water." (*Zach.* 9:11).

Chapter 13

A Voice in the Concert
Of the Elect

WEEKS before the tidal wave of green sweeps upward from the South, the sap that produces vegetation has been flowing unseen in root and trunk and branches, that now under the warm sun disclose a land of promise. So also the divine sap of Christ's Precious Blood had been flowing from those sacred springs on Mount Calvary through the arteries of the infant Church before its fruits blossomed forth under the warmth of the fiery tongues of Pentecost. This vital fluid has ever been the divine life of the Church from the moment of its creation. Throughout the centuries and in every part of the globe, it circulates through the channels of the sacraments in the veins of the mystical body of Christ. Hence the Church is a living organism with the divine life of the Precious Blood and the Holy Ghost insuring its indefectibility and indestructibility.

Once Our Lord sat at the well of Jacob and said to the Samaritan woman: "If thou didst know the gift of God, and who is he that saith to thee, give me to drink; thou perhaps wouldst have asked of him, and he would have given thee living water." (*John* 4:10). Here natural water was drawn from the earth to slake the thirst of the body. Now Jesus in the Tabernacle is sitting at

86

a thousand wells of salvation in His Church and offering us drink from the soul-nourishing stream of His Sacred Heart.

Christ, the same yesterday, today, and forever, continues to live in His Church, both as Shepherd and as Lamb. As Shepherd, He watches over His flock and carries the lost sheep upon His shoulders; as Lamb, He lays down His life for His own, and offers His very flesh and blood to His followers.

Thus, too, the ministers of the Church have ever proved themselves both shepherd and lamb, and the blood of martyrs has always been the seed of Christianity. According to the divine plan, we must all become lambs, we "must become as little children" before we can grow into heroes. "He that loveth this life shall lose it; and he that hateth his life in this world, keepeth it unto life eternal." (*John* 12:25).

Christ came to conquer; but He conquered by becoming a lamb and shedding His Blood for us; then He arose as the Lion of the tribe of Juda. His Wounds and His Blood became the panoply of His beauty and strength, as the prophet Isaias had foretold: "Who is this that cometh from Edom, with dyed garments from Bosra, this beautiful one in his robe, walking in the greatness of his strength." (*Is.* 63:1).

The trophies of the Precious Blood are souls saved and sanctified. For this purpose it was shed. We must not be scandalized in Jesus Christ, or allow ourselves to be dispersed like sheep, when the enemy shall strike the shepherd. "Blessed is he that shall not be scandalized in me."

The magnificent procession of the Precious Blood in the holy Sacrifice of the Mass over the entire earth, every twenty-four hours, is one continual triumph of the Blood of Calvary, and the refulgence of the Precious Blood from 300,000 chalices is far more beautiful to the

Most High, than the golden sunset is to us here on earth. It is so consoling to see that this adorable Blood has not been shed in vain, that it is truly raised on our altars *"in remissionem peccatorum."* Who can recount the triumphs of the Precious Blood in the confessional? Who can conceive their number and greatness? They are partially revealed at the communion railing. What glorious fruits of the Precious Blood can be observed at every successful mission!

But the principal part of the divine work of the Precious Blood is hidden in the secrecy of souls, and there are countless triumphs of truth and grace which will never be known till the day of judgment. The very greatest sacrifices we must make are hidden from the gaze of the world. The heaviest crosses have always been those which we must drag along, unseen by human eyes, and the bitterest struggles of all are fought in the stillness of the heart. The spiritual and hidden life of Christians has been the scene of fiercer battles and greater victories than those which have been recorded in the history of the world.

These are triumphs of the Precious Blood. They will come to light on the day of judgment.This day will witness the rich harvest of the Blood of Calvary. Our Saviour will appear with His Five Wounds radiant, and the bodies of the just will reflect the glory of their Redeemer. "But the Lord shall rise upon thee, and His glory shall be seen upon thee." (*Is.* 60:2).

Oh, what honor, what glory, what ecstacy of joy, to belong after the final judgment to that interminable army, that countless phalanx of patriarchs and prophets, apostles and martyrs, virgins and confessors, of holy souls and glorified bodies, leaving forever this earth, the place of their trials and struggles, singing paeans of praise, and following Our Lord and His Blessed Mother and the angels into everlasting happiness!

St. John saw this final triumph of the Precious Blood when he wrote: "[Thou] hast redeemed us, to our God, in thy blood, out of every tribe and tongue and people and nation, And thou hast made us to our God a kingdom." (*Apoc.* 5:9-10).

This is the burden of the triumphal song of the elect in Heaven. "Thou has redeemed us, O Lord God, in thy blood." They have become "kings" because they have conquered the world, the kingdom of Satan, "and they overcame him by the blood of the Lamb." They refer all the glory of Heaven to the merits of the Blood of the Lamb. "The Lamb that was slain is worthy to receive power and divinity, and wisdom, and strength, and glory, and benediction." Devotion to the Precious Blood will burst forth in all its glory in Heaven from "harp" and "golden viols" and in "new canticles" and with "loud voices" and the number of them "will be thousands of thousands." (*Apoc.* 5:8, 9, 11). Glory be to the Blood of Jesus now and forever and throughout all ages, for it was not shed in vain!

"I saw great multitudes which no man could number." These are the fruits of the Precious Blood, these bear witness to its infinite mercies. "Clothed with white robes and palms in their hands." White is the emblem of purity and holiness; palms are the signs of victory. All the palms that the Blessed carry in their hands grew along the stream of the Precious Blood; all the crowns that adorn their heads were made from laurel watered by the refreshing dew of the Precious Blood; all the glory in which the elect shine in Heaven, is a reflection of the ruddy glow of the Precious Blood. "And he said to me: 'These are they who are come out of great tribulation, and have washed their robes and have made them white in the blood of the Lamb.'" (*Apoc.* 7:14). Thus St. John bears testimony that no one enters Heaven unless he has come out of great tribulation here on earth; in other words, "no cross, no crown." We often hear persons remark: "No one knows how much I suffer." Ah! your sufferings are not only known and understood in Heaven, but they are openly proclaimed as the cause of your joy. "These are they who are come out of great tribulation."

But we must also observe what follows: "And have washed their robes and have made them white in the blood of the Lamb." This they have done by the laver of holy Baptism, then by the Sacrament of Penance, and the garments thus made white, they have beautified still more by frequent Holy Communion and the reception of the other sacraments. "Therefore," continues the ancient, speaking to St. John in Heaven, "they are before the throne of God. The Lamb which is in the midst of the throne, shall rule them and shall lead them to the fountains of the waters of life, and God shall wipe away all tears from their eyes." Here on earth they "sat and wept when they remembered Sion." Now they shall drink from the torrent of delights, flowing from the fountains of salvation.

"And the city hath no need of the sun, nor the moon, to shine in it. For the glory of God hath enlightened it, and the Lamb is the lamp thereof." (*Apoc.* 21:23). Having seen the "bride of the Lamb" which is the throng of the elect, St. John then describes the Holy City and the Lamb that rules it. "There must be a particular significance attached to the word *Lamb* in this passage," writes Mgsr. Adalbert Huhn, "that St. John did not simply mention Jesus Christ, the Son of God, as forming the center of light of the heavenly Jerusalem." "The Lamb that was slain," that died and rose again as "the lion of the tribe of Juda" with the marks of death in His Five Wounds radiant with glory, the Lamb as the symbol of life and death, as the emblem of the Precious Blood standing for victim and victory, this is the meaning underlying the word Lamb in Scripture. Isaias speaks of the Saviour not only as a "lamb that shall be dumb before his shearer." (*Is.* 53:7), but also as a conqueror: "Send forth, O Lord, the Lamb, the ruler of the earth." (*Is.* 16:1). St. John the Baptist points out our Saviour by the name of Lamb; "Behold the Lamb of God that takes away the sins of the world." But how does the Lamb take away the sins of the world? By His Blood. "This is he that came by water and blood, Jesus Christ." (*1 John* 5:6). Our holy mother, the Church, always in closest touch with the Scriptures, has taken this name from the lips of the great prophet Isaias and from the two Johns, so near and dear to Our Lord, and with this endearing name addresses her divine Spouse at Mass before Communion: "Lamb of God who taketh away the sins of the world, have mercy on us, give us peace," or "grant them eternal rest." It is also the appellation we give Our Lord in all the litanies. The Lamb of God, of His own free will shedding His Blood for us, is the greatest proof of God's love and mercy for us; the Lamb of God enthroned upon our altars with the holy and ever memorable Wounds characteristic of His death will forever occupy the throne of the Most High in Heaven as the greatest living memorial of the Holy Trinity for mankind redeemed. The Five Wounds are Our Lord's greatest ornaments in Heaven and like five brilliant suns they illuminate the eternal mansions.

"Blessed are they that are called to the marriage supper of the Lamb." (*Apoc.* 19:9). There they shall find the Holy Grail, the living Chalice of the Precious Blood that fills the earth with grace, hearts with peace and consolation, the graves with hope, and Heaven with glory. There all shall be filled with the delight of the "Chalice of Benediction," which was even here on earth "a communication of the Blood of Christ." "They shall be inebriated with the plenty of thy house; and thou shalt make them drink of the torrent of thy pleasure. For with thee is the fountain of life; and in thy light we shall see light." (*Ps.* 35:9-10).

Although still mourning and weeping in this valley of tears, with St. Paul I shall repeat again and again, "I have 'confidence in the entering into the holies by the blood of Christ.'" (*Heb.* 10:19). The prophet Isaias writes of the coming Redeemer: "Behold, I have graven thee in my hands." "And wherewith hast Thou engraven me in Thy hands?" asks St. Augustine, and then he himself replies: "With the Blood of Thy Sacred Wounds." Then he continues confidently, "See, O Lord, come and read this handwriting and let me enter into Thy glory."

Merciful Jesus, Thou didst not withhold from me one drop of Thy Blood; how couldst Thou then refuse me entrance into Heaven? The mercy of Thy Precious Blood endureth from generation to generation. By the bloody sweat of Thy agony, grant me, I beseech Thee, the grace of a perfect contrition before I die.

With the liquid fire of Thy Sacred Heart consume all my iniquities and wipe out all my hidden sins. Let me die a victim of Thy love that I may sing Thy mercies forever and ever!

Devotion to the Precious Blood

PART II

Chapter 1

Devotion to the Precious Blood

ITS NATURE AND PRACTICE

ALTHOUGH the Blood of Jesus, even when separated from His Body in the Passion was divine and adorable by reason of the hypostatic union with the Divinity, devotion to the Precious Blood does not now consist in the veneration of the material, corporal Blood separated from His Body or sprinkled over His limbs, His garments, or the instruments of His Passion.

The immediate object of this devotion is, first and foremost, Jesus Christ, who has redeemed us with His Blood; "Christum Dei Filium, qui suo nos redemit Sanguine, venite adoremus."

If we should turn away from the person of Jesus Christ and venerate His Sacred Blood apart from Him who shed it out of love for us, our devotion would be false and would lead to all kinds of extravagance. In all such devotions Jesus Christ Himself must be the central figure of our thoughts and our worship.

In our devotion to the Precious Blood, therefore, we represent to ourselves Jesus Christ in the livery of His Passion, His Sacred Blood oozing from every pore and trickling to the ground in the Garden of Gethsemani;

we think of Him at the Pillar of Scourging, His Body torn with lashes and covered with Blood, like a "Garment sprinkled with blood;" we "behold the Man" before the Pretorium with the Blood of the Crowning with Thorns reddening His pale temples, pouring over His face and neck, and dropping down on the tattered robe of mockery; we follow to Golgotha the bleeding Cross-bearer, marking the royal way of the Cross with His Blood; standing beneath the Cross, we worship Our Saviour in the greatest ardor of His love, in the very act of accomplishing our redemption, and we contemplate with a contrite and grateful heart the fountains of salvation opened in His sacred hands and feet and side, and sending forth streams of mercy and love to cleanse, to heal and to nourish the weak and sinful soul of fallen man.

From the fact that Our Lord appears to saintly souls here on earth with His Blood flowing from His thorn-crowned head and His five wounds, we may infer that He is pleased to have us contemplate Him thus in the devotion to His Precious Blood. With regard to those who received the stigmata, or bloody wounds of Our Saviour's Passion, in their bodies, the learned Father Poulain, S.J., writes: "As a rule, they had visions in keeping with the part of fellow-sufferers with Jesus Christ: Our Lord showing Himself to them in the blood-stained garments of His Passion."

This devotion has for its chief object Him Who "cometh from Edom, with dyed garments from Bosra, this beautiful one in his robe, walking in the greatness of his strength," as the Prophet Isaias (*Is.* 63:1) had foreseen Him aflame with love as a combating hero gaining a victory for our freedom in His Blood. "In the imperishable and roseate adornment of His bleeding wounds, Our Lord reveals the inextinguishable flames of love that burn for us in His merciful

Heart." "Behold and consider the rose of the bloody passion, how it glows as a mark of the most ardent love. Love and suffering contend with each other: love, to burn more; suffering, to bleed more. The rose of love would be crimsoned in suffering, and the rose of suffering would glow in the fire of love. Behold, how in this rosy attire our best vine bloomed, Jesus crimsoned with Blood! Consider His whole Body, and see if you do not recognize the bloom of the blood-red rose! Look at one hand and then at the other, do you not observe the red rose in each? Behold one foot and then the other, are they not rose-colored? Contemplate the pierced side, the rose is not wanting there. Oh what a stream of Blood flowed from the deep wounds of His Sacred Body! In this fount (of His Sacred Body) our rose is dyed and glows in deepest crimson hues; for most ardently did love's fire burn when suffering revealed itself in crimson red. In the greatness of the torment you behold the greatness of love. The Rose glitters with a twofold light before you—it is fiery in its love, and blood-red in its suffering. By the flames of love, suffering is purpled; for if there were no love, there would not be this suffering. And again—from this blood-red of torment, love radiates in its fullness and glory." St. Bernard.

It was the Blood of Jesus Christ, shed upon the Cross, that was the immediate cause of the redemption of mankind. The words of the great Apostle are as follows: *"Sine sanguinis effusione non fit remissio"*—"without shedding of blood there is no remission." (*Heb.* 9:22). And elsewhere, in a still more explicit manner: *"In quo habemus redemptionem per sanguinem ejus, remissionem peccatorum"*—"In whom we have redemption through His Blood, the remission of sins." (*Col.* 1:14). Devotion to the Precious Blood, therefore, must be focused on the great Sacrifice of the Cross, the culmination of Our Lord's life and mission here on earth.

Now the Holy Sacrifice of the Mass is a renewal of Our Lord's bloody passion and death on the Cross. "When, at the Last Supper, Jesus converted bread and wine into His Sacred Body and Blood, He did not change both at the same time, nor under one form, but changed each separately, and under two distinct forms. He might have said the words: 'This is My Body and My Blood' over the bread; had He done so, the bread would have been truly His living Body and Blood, but He would not thus have manifested His death to us in so clear a manner. He chose, therefore, first to change the bread only, by virtue of the words of consecration, into His Sacred Body and give it to His disciples to eat, and afterwards the wine into His Sacred Blood, and give it also separately to His disciples. And by the guidance of the Holy Spirit He has taught His Church to ordain that the priest should first change the Bread into His Sacred Body, and elevate it, and then proceed to change the wine into His Blood, and elevate that also separately to bring His death more definitely before the minds of the people.

"On this subject Lancicius says: 'Because, in the order of nature, dissolution follows upon the total separation of the blood from the body, this being the immediate cause of Christ's death upon the Cross, the manner in which He chose to accomplish the sacrifice of Himself, therefore, in the holy sacrifice of the Mass His death is likewise set forth by the separation of His Blood from His Body. Thus by the words of consecration His Body becomes present under the form of the bread, His Blood beneath that of the wine, each distinct and apart from the other.' This is a true immolation of Christ wherein the substances of bread and wine are changed and annihilated."—Cochem.

In the Mass, the Precious Blood of Christ is mystically shed for us, it cries for mercy and pleads for us, our souls are sprinkled with it, and it is offered as a sweet odor in the sight of God. In all this, as well as in the separate consecration of the chalice at Mass, we have a reason for a particular devotion to the Precious Blood.

Hence, devotion to the Precious Blood leads us, in the second place, to the holy sacrifice of the Mass, the center of Catholic worship, and teaches us a better appreciation of the Eucharistic Blood of Christ.

In His Passion Our Lord's "apparel was red," and in the Church his "garments are still like theirs that tread in the winepress," because in the Mass Christ is "always living to make intercession for us" (*Heb.* 7:25) is continually offered, not merely by the word of the priest, nor by the elevation of the Adorable Sacrament, but in a manner in which He mystically suffers, is immolated and slain. St. Gregory says: "Although Christ dies not again, yet He suffers again for us in the sacrifice of the Mass after a mysterious, mystical manner." "For although in Holy Mass Christ does not suffer physical pain or death, yet He displays Himself to His Heavenly Father under the same pitiable appearance which He presented when scourged, crowned with thorns, and crucified; and this as distinctly as if He were again enduring these tortures in reality for the sins of the world."

"The Church, as well as every follower of Christ, must here below pass through her Holy Week, must endure a bloody sweat on the Mount of Olives, and upon Calvary she must abide the torment of the Cross, she must struggle and combat, labor and suffer, endure and bleed; in a word, like Our Lord's life, hers, too, must be a constant sacrifice of love and sacrifice of suffering. The bloody and unbloody martyrdom is a prominent feature and a special characteristic of the

Catholic Church, by which she resembles her Divine
Master and Founder, and is distinguished from all religious sects."

"The Sacrifice of the Cross is the primary source,
which, at the altar in the Mass, gushes forth anew day
by day, to refill continually the channels of the Sacraments which bring to us the saving waters of redemption. Inasmuch as on the altar the same Sacrifice is
offered as was offered on the Cross, we may designate
the Mass also as the Sacrificial source whence flow
the Sacramental streams of grace and salvation.

"Like the Sacraments, the Sacramentals are also
connected with the Eucharistic Sacrifice and source of
blessing, from which they, in a certain sense, draw
their salutary efficacy; for on the altar in the Holy
Mass that stream of Blood and water from Golgotha
continues to flow, in whose flood the earth, the sea,
the starry firmament, in a word, the universe is
cleansed, that is, touched with the blessing of Redemption and led on to its future transformation: *"Unda
manat et cruor: terra, pontus, astra mundus quo lavantur flumine!"* (Hymn. Eccl.).

"Blood," says St. Thomas, "is more specially the image
of Our Lord's Passion than the Body." Hence devotion
to the Precious Blood is eminently designed to bring
home to our minds and hearts Our Saviour's great love
for us in His Passion and in the Mass. "I lay down my
life for my sheep." This Our Lord does constantly in
the Eucharistic Sacrifice.

Devotion to the Precious Blood receives its inspiration from Holy Writ; from Genesis to the Apocalypse,
from the Patriarch Jacob, who prophesies of the Messias: "He shall wash his robes in wine, and his garment in the blood of the grape." (*Gen.* 49:11), to St.
John who writes: "Blessed are they that wash their
robes in the blood of the Lamb: that they may have a

right to the tree of life, and may enter in by the gates into the city." (*Apoc.* 22:14).

Jesus shed His Sacred Blood that we may have more abundant life. "And of His fullness we have all received." His Precious Blood is a divine gulf stream that changes the climate of our cold and barren hearts, and fills them with the breath of Heaven, making them throb with divine love, and rendering them a paradise of virtues.

"Ravishingly beautiful is the garden of the Church, where 'bloom the violets of humility, where the lilies of purity shine brightly and roses of martyrdom glow.' But whence do these noble, heavenly plants draw their life's sap, their nourishment, their growth, their perfume and their bright colors? Chiefly from the Eucharistic Sacrifice and fountain of grace. The fountains of the Saviour which in the garden of the Church unceasingly flow on thousands of altars, irrigate and fructify the soul, refresh and strengthen the tender shoots, and cause the seed of virtue to blossom and ripen. If the just man flourishes like the palm and is likened unto a tree planted near running waters, and producing fruit in due season, all this to be attributed principally to the stream of grace issuing from the Sacrifice of the Mass. Christian perfection must be acquired and be preserved by the spirit of sacrifice and the supernatural, heroic spirit of sacrifice can be drawn only from this perennial fountain."—Gihr.

"The world idly suffers itself to be fairly inundated with blessings, without asking where the fountain of these blessings is, just like the Egyptians who allow the Nile to irrigate their lands, without inquiring for its source."

"And I, if I be lifted up from the earth, will draw all things to myself." (*John* 12:32). The power of Jesus to attract souls has not waned during the centuries, rather it is seen to increase in sweetness and effectiveness. In the language of Isaias, Our Lord expects us to "draw water with joy out of the Saviour's fountains." But people must first be brought to these fountains of living water which are found in the Sacrifice of the Mass and in the Sacraments. It is here that our Saviour draws all hearts to Himself. "You were at that time without Christ, being aliens from the conversation of Israel and strangers to the testament, having no hope of the promise, and without God in this world. But now in Christ Jesus, you, who sometime were afar off, are made nigh by the blood of Christ." (*Eph.* 2:12-13).

Now it is the business of the Precious Blood Devotion to bring us nigh to the Blood of Christ; to stimulate in the hearts of the faithful a special devotion to the Most Precious Blood of Jesus by holding out to them its power of sanctification, expiation, protection and intercession; to apply the infinite merits of the Blood of the Atonement to our own souls and to those of others; to excite in our hearts a spirit of reparation for the coldness and indifference of men toward the Price of our Redemption; and to fill us with a lively love for Jesus and gratitude towards him, "Who loves us and washed us in His Blood."

The spirit of reparation must always be a chief characteristic of the Precious Blood Devotion, just as it is a prominent feature of the Devotion to the Sacred Heart. The constant yearning which seems to have consumed Our Lord with a burning desire to shed His Blood for us long before His hour had come and which is expressed in those loving words: "and I have a baptism wherewith I am to be baptized: and how am I straitened until it be accomplished." (*Luke* 12:50), must find a responsive chord in our hearts if we are not entirely insensible to divine love, and it must awaken in our souls a desire to glorify and adore our bleeding

Saviour in the very act of His dying for love of us.

The Devotion to the Precious Blood is truly apostolic in its results, and will prove a wonderful power for moral regeneration in a parish. What could give greater fecundity to souls created by God than the Blood of the Son of God? What could produce in the soil thus fructified a richer harvest than the divine rain of Christ's own Blood? "When the priest, offering the highest act of worship, elevates the sacred host and the chalice, the blood of our God distills from them like a gentle rain from the clouds, bedewing not the earth, not the bodies of men, but the souls and minds of all who are present. Nor is its gracious influence confined to the good and pious; it is extended also to the evil. The souls of the just it purifies and embellishes; it makes them fruitful in good works, it strengthens them when they are weak, it subdues the force of temptation, it effects in them all the good of which each one is capable. Those who are not devout Christians, it seeks to convert, to soften their hearts, to correct their evil inclinations; while to all who are enemies of God it offers peace and reconciliation. And for the sinner who, in his obduracy resists the proffered grace, the Precious Blood pleads with God for him and arrests the arm of justice."

The field for the Blood of the Redeemer is the entire world, but its application must be made to every human being. A pious writer tells us: "That which on the cross was a sacrifice of redemption is in Holy Mass a sacrifice of appropriation, whereby the virtue and the power of the sacrifice of the cross is applied to each one individually." All need the ministration of the Precious Blood: the hundred millions of heathens, the millions of heretics, the millions of sinners, the many souls in danger of mortal sin, the countless lukewarm Christians, the hosts of souls striving after perfection, the hundred thousand dying daily, the suffering souls in Purgatory.

All the faithful of both sexes can offer up the Precious Blood for these intentions; for it is written: "[Thou] hast made us to our God a kingdom and priests." (*Apoc.* 5:10).

In the oblation of the all-saving Blood of Jesus lies the practical part of the Devotion to the Precious Blood. "The value of the Sacrifice of the Mass consists in offering it to God. The faithful should not merely assist, praying while the Victim is immolated, but with the priest they should offer the Sacrifice. That they have this power the Church expressly tells them when the priest says: 'Pray, brethren, that my sacrifice, which is also yours, may be acceptable to God the Father Almighty.' And again, after the Sanctus: 'Remember, O Lord, Thy servants here present, for whom we offer, and who offer for themselves, and all men.' Will you neglect the use of your mystical priesthood for yourselves and others, for the salvation of the world, and the glory of God?"

It should be a part of the object of this devotion to unfold to the faithful the priceless treasures of the Mass and to make them hungry and thirsty for the supernatural. "All you that thirst, come to the waters: and you that have no money make haste, buy and eat: come ye, buy wine and milk without money and without any price." (*Is.* 55:1).

The Eucharistic Blood should be offered to God first as a sacrifice of adoration and praise, as a libation to our sovereign Ruler. St. Paul says: "Christ hath loved us, and hath delivered Himself for us, an oblation, and a sacrifice to God for an odor of sweetness." (*Eph.* 5:2). The death of mortal man is accompanied by an odor of decay; but the mystical death of Christ in the Mass is a sweet odor of love and praise to all Heaven.

The Chalice with the Blood of Christ should be offered

as a sacrifice of thanksgiving. Just before he consumes the Sacred Blood in the Mass the priest says: "What shall I render to the Lord for all he hath rendered unto me? I will take the chalice of salvation, and call upon the name of the Lord." One day, while in ecstacy, St. Mary Magdalen de Pazzi exclaimed: "Every time a creature offers to God the Precious Blood with which he was redeemed, he presents Him with a gift of inestimable value."

The Precious Blood is pre-eminently a sacrifice of propitiation. "Whom God hath proposed to be a propitiation, through faith in his blood." (*Rom.* 3:25). Its power and efficacy extend to sins, punishments and satisfaction. By her prayers the Church teaches us the importance of first appeasing the anger of God on account of our sins and ingratitude toward Him before we appeal to Him for graces and favors from His mercy. We are all poor sinners deserving punishment rather than favors, but when we interpose the Blood of Jesus, the Blood of reconciliation, between God and us, the heavenly Father cannot but be merciful to us.

The Precious Blood pleads for us in the Mass, and how consoling is this voice of impetration! You are "come to Jesus the mediator of the new testament, and to the sprinkling of blood which speaketh better than that of Abel." (*Heb.* 12:24). You wish to obtain some particular favor, but your prayers are weak; then let the voice of this Divine Blood plead for you, for "It speaketh better than that of Abel," and the voice of his blood was heard in Heaven. In spirit take the chalice with the Eucharistic Blood, the same Blood that Jesus shed on the Cross, and holding it aloft, plead your cause with the Blood of the Atonement in your hands; or ask the Sorrowful Mother, who stood beneath the Cross when the Blood of her dying Son was dripping from His wounds, to make the offering and inter-

cede for you. That which opened Heaven for us cannot fail to obtain for us all the treasures of Heaven.

"The water that flows from the snowcapped moun-
tains, the torrents that descend, forming streams and
rivers, now fertilize fields, energize industry, facilitate
commerce, and benefit the whole world. Under this
apparent sterility and death, energy and force were
hidden and dormant, waiting until men were ready
and able to use them. Wherever this force is carried,
it produces wonderful results. It descends from the
high solitudes into the plains, and all the industries
of the world drink from these springs whose source is
so near the heavens. Many unbelieving and indifferent souls regard the Mass as unnecessary; many Christians, even, go to Mass without fully understanding
its great worth and merit, or appreciating its value;
they do not know that under this appearance of death
and nothingness, are hidden the fullness of Strength
and Life. They do not know that from those heights of
Calvary which reach to Heaven, torrents of grace and
benediction flow upon the world. They ignore the treasures of activity, of felicity, of fruitfulness, of unlimited progress for the moral and supernatural life of
the entire human race contained in every Mass. They
know not that the very life of God and His omnipo-
tence are placed, through the Mass, at the disposal of
men, and await only their good will to render them
the most marvelous and divine service, for the mili-
tant here, for the suffering souls in Purgatory, and the
elect in Paradise; for earth and for Heaven, for God's
own glory, and for the salvation of the world."

The Precious Blood Devotion prompts us to direct
the streams of life-giving Blood in the thousands of
chalices upon our altars into the hearts of men, obtain-
ing for one the light of faith or grace of conversion;
encouraging some tender and vacillating soul to fol-

low the calling to the priesthood or religious state; preventing some unholy alliance here and urging others on to good there. Who can measure the extent of good that can be accomplished by utilizing the channels of superabundant life on our altars?

How many millions of sins are committed every day, whereby the love and the goodness of God is outraged! By offering up the Precious Blood of Jesus daily, to save the sorely tempted from falling into sin, what untold honor and glory may we not give to the majesty and holiness of God! This act of love and zeal will be at the same time a means of atonement for our own sins, and will strengthen us in the love of God. Perhaps you have a father, a brother, a sister, a friend, who has fallen by the wayside. The path from the Good Shepherd to the lost sheep is sprinkled, as it were, with the Blood of the God-Man. Plead that this Blood may not have been shed in vain. "He must know that he who causeth a sinner to be converted from the error of his way, shall save his soul from death, and shall cover a multitude of sins." (*Jas.* 5:20).

It is estimated that about 100,000 persons die daily. How many of these are lost? Can you not, for the love of God, by your daily oblations, clothe one of these souls with the purple of Christ's redeeming Blood? One of the principal reasons why the Agony of Jesus in Gethsemani was so intense that it made Him shed tears of Blood from every pore of His Sacred Body, was that he foresaw how many souls would be lost, even after He had spilt every drop of His Blood for them. "And he was clothed with a garment sprinkled with blood; and his name is called, The Word of God." (*Apoc.* 19:13).

Christ shed His Blood for all men that all might be saved; and yet, for want of missionary help, there are hundreds of millions of human beings, who have not yet received the Gospel message. How many there are in our own land, our very neighbors, whom we know and love, who are entirely ignorant of the Price of our Redemption! The missionary field is preeminently the domain of the Precious Blood. If more souls are not saved it is because we are remiss in our oblations of the Precious Blood in their behalf. "It is to be feared," exclaimed St. Magdalen de Pazzi, "that the impenitence of sinners is in proportion to our idleness. Oh! if we would offer in their behalf the Blood of Our Saviour, God would be reconciled to them and save them."

Jesus is daily offering the best He has, His own lifeblood, by shedding, mystically, on the altar, that same Blood which He poured out for us all on the Cross. With bleeding hands, as it were, He is admonishing us that "the harvest is ripe" but that "the laborers are few." The ransom Christ paid for our brothers and sisters yet sitting in darkness, is present on our altars in abundance, but it must be applied to souls by means of oblation and ministration. God wants our co-operation, and, at our intercession, will bestow extraordinary graces, through the merits of His Precious Blood, upon the efforts of the missionaries—graces, without which, they may labor in vain, because "Faith is a gift that cometh by prayer."

How dear to the Sacred Heart must be an oblation of the Precious Blood for the fulfillment of its ardent desire and prayer that there may be "one fold and one shepherd!" Truly, the Apostolate of the Precious Blood should be promoted everywhere, because Christ has left this priceless treasure in abundance for the ransom of souls.

Offering the Blood of Jesus in expiation for the suffering souls in Purgatory is the most efficacious means at our disposal to help those holy souls. At times God permits souls from Purgatory to appear to the living, to plead personally for help, and there is nothing for which they beg so pitifully and so ardently, as for the Blood of the Holy Sacrifice. This Divine Blood was shed, and is offered daily at the altar, for the remission of sin, and for the remission of the punishment due to sin. The Blood of Jesus in the Mass falls like dew upon the suffering souls, refreshing and consoling them.

The more we think and reflect on this subject, the more convinced we become that the Precious Blood Devotion is not merely beautiful in its nature, springing from the wounds of Our Saviour and flowing out of the very life of the Church, but that it is eminently practical, fruitful, and truly apostolic, resembling in its effectiveness the mighty but silent forces of nature.

Chapter 2

A Devotion For
Every Christian

THE devotion to the Precious Blood is not a devotion for a few chosen souls who desire to accumulate particular merits, but one which should be cherished and practiced with love and gratitude by every soul that wishes to be saved. Christ shed His Blood for all men; hence there is no human being who does not owe a debt of gratitude to this Price of our Redemption. "Knowing that you were not redeemed with corruptible things as gold and silver . . . but with the precious blood of Christ." (*1 Ptr.* 1:18). Therefore, if we reach Heaven at all, it will be because we are clothed with the "dyed garments from Bosra," with the Blood of our Redemption. "But now in Christ Jesus, you, who some time were afar off, are made nigh by the blood of Christ." (*Eph.* 2:13).

There are some, perhaps, who are more repelled than attracted by the very name of the devotion to the Precious Blood. The word blood easily suggests pain and death—the two things most dreaded by human nature. "The life of the flesh is in the blood," and to see blood flowing fills us instinctively with horror.

When Jesus promised to give us His flesh to eat and His Blood to drink, we know that "Many therefore of his disciples, hearing it, said: 'This saying is hard, and

110

who can hear it?' But Jesus, knowing in himself that his disciples murmured at this, said to them: 'Doth this scandalize you? It is the spirit that quickeneth.'" (*John* 6:61-62, 64).

It is true that the devotion to the Precious Blood does remind us of pain inflicted, and a life that was sacrified; but it leads us directly to the source of love and salvation, to Calvary where the fountains of the Saviour were opened, and to the Altar where these fountains are ever flowing, in the holy Sacrifice of the Mass.

It brings home to our minds that the Blood which we see flowing is divine, since it is being shed for us by the God-Man, Who came to redeem us in His Blood. It leads us to the foot of the Cross where it causes us to exclaim in the words of St. John: "God so loved the world!"

Therefore, while this devotion does contain an element of wholesome fear, by arousing in us the consciousness of our guilt, and awakening within our hearts deep sorrow for our sins, it also produces in our souls that generous love which arouses the spirit of self-abnegation and causes us to emulate Him whose love for us led to the Supreme Sacrifice. "Greater love than this no man hath, that a man lay down his life for his friends. (*John* 15:13).

Devotion to the Precious Blood brings us face to face with two fundamental doctrines of our holy religion: fallen man in all his misery, shut out from Paradise and Heaven, "mourning and weeping in this valley of tears;" and Jesus, the Son of the living God, restoring the child of perdition to the dignity of a child of God and heir to Heaven. An angel with a flaming sword guards the entrance to Paradise lost; but Jesus, in the crimson garment of His Blood, all flame with love, reopens the gate of Heaven for us.

A religion that is divorced from these basic truths is like a nut that lacks a kernel. In our age of luxury and religious indifference, men do not care to be reminded of a moral regeneration, of struggling against the flesh, the world and the devil; they do not wish to hear of their obligation to make use of the means of salvation, and thus cooperate with God's grace. This effeminate world loathes a Church in which the Cross occupies a prominent place, and in which the Crucified is adored, and implored for mercy.

Solid piety, and genuine and lasting devotion, however, must be founded upon the dogmas of the Church, and be rooted in a spirit of sacrifice and self-abasement. It should consist in the love of God and His Church, and be productive of practical charity, and a willingness to undergo sufferings, in submission to Divine Providence; otherwise, our devotions are in danger of becoming whimsical, and of degenerating into mere sentimentalism. "They have forsaken me, the fountain of living water, and have digged to themselves cisterns, broken cisterns, that can hold no water." (*Jer.* 2:13).

While Moses was upon the mountain praying, and receiving the Ten Commandments, the fickle-minded Israelites were dancing around a golden calf of their own making. The vagaries of men's minds can never replace the revealed truths of God; neither can the outward forms of piety be a substitute for real and practical religion.

He who is so fastidious in his religious tastes as to feel an aversion to the contemplation or worship of Christ in His Blood, clearly shows that he is wanting in the true love of Jesus. "The sweet serenity, the profound calm, the silence, interior suffering, the divine majesty of the Sacred Face" of our Saviour in His Passion is ever, to the devout soul, and object of

love and holy inspiration. "We preach Christ crucified, unto the Jews indeed a stumbling block, and
unto the Gentiles foolishness; but unto them that are
called, both Jews and Greeks, Christ the power of
God, and the wisdom of God. For the foolishness of
God is wiser than men; and the weakness of God is
stronger than men." (*1 Cor.* 1:23-25).

Robert Hugh Benson, in "A Book of the Love of Jesus,"
writes: "It is supposed to be a mark of modern deli-
cacy and spiritual instinct, to despise and shrink from
realism; to dwell upon the Risen Christ, the robed and
crowned King, or upon the stainless Child of Bethlehem, and to avoid the vision of the blood-stained Man
of Sorrows with His torn limbs. But the true mystic
reads the awfulness of sin in the awfulness of the
Cross—the story of his own life written so carefully
and accurately in blood over the white body and soul
of his Saviour—and he sees the infinite love of God in
the infinite suffering that He so willingly undertook;
the full fragrance of the Beloved is not perceptible
except when He is bruised and torn."

Is not the blood in our veins the source of life and
joy and beauty? What fills the eye with brightness and
luster? What flushes our cheeks like the blush of the
newborn day? What purples our lips with ruby gems?
What gives us a feeling of youth, imparting elasticity
to the limb and buoyancy to the heart? Pure and rich
blood. Right and abstemious living, simple and wholesome food, timely and healthful exercise—all tend to
produce pure and rich blood, and to regulate its cir-
culation through the body. In the spiritual order, devotion to the Precious Blood is one of the means which
give a healthy pulse to our piety.

"And they showed the elephants the blood of grapes
. . . to provoke them to fight." (*1 Mach.* 6:34). Should
not the Blood of the Son of God, the Conqueror of

Satan, the Hero of our salvation, fill us likewise with new spiritual life and hope and courage? The love of Jesus that crimsoned His Body seven times with the color of roses will quicken our eyes of faith, cover our cheeks with the glow of devotion, render our lips eloquent with the praises of God, warm our hearts with the fire of divine love and cause us to walk unfalteringly in the footprints of Jesus. Among these beautiful words with which St. Agnes, one of the most heroic and glorious of the early martyrs, spurned the son of the pro-consul and uttered her burning love for Jesus Crucified, are the following: *"Sanguis ejus ornavit genas meas."* "His Blood hath adorned my cheeks."

Oh, that divine gulf stream of the Precious Blood which flowed from Calvary and which, in the language of the Church, *"mira tandem vis amoris, lavit orbem flumine,"* "His Blood hath adorned my cheeks."

Oh, that divine gulf stream of the Precious Blood which flowed from Calvary and which, in the language of the Church, *"mira tandem vis amoris, lavit orbem flumine,"* bathed the entire globe, must reach all hearts! Then they shall possess the climate of the Sacred Heart of Jesus; they shall be filled with its warmth and love and beauty, and be fertile with heavenly virtues.

Chapter 3

The Devotion
Of the Elect

T HE rites and sacrifices of blood prescribed by God in the Old Law, and foreshadowing the Blood of the Lamb of God in the New Testament, were the chief forms of worship of the chosen people from the beginning. The holy sacrifice of the Mass, in which wine is changed into the Blood of Christ, is a continuation of the bloody sacrifice of Calvary, where Christ fulfilled the figurative meaning of the bloody victims of the past.

At the Last Supper, Christ took the cup and declared in a solemn manner: "This is the chalice, the new testament in my blood."(*Luke* 22:20). The Apostles were commanded to do as He had done, to change wine into the Blood of Christ. "Do this in commemoration of me." These words imply an invitation to remember Him in His Blood on the Cross, for the Eucharist is a memorial of His Passion. The Church will continue to go down the ages till the end of time, holding aloft the chalice of Blood for our adoration and propitiation. "For as often as you shall eat this bread, and drink the chalice, you shall show the death of the Lord until He come." (*1 Cor.* 11:26).

St. Peter reminds us of the eternal decree—"foreknown indeed before the foundation of the world"—

the inestimable value of the Precious Blood, and the
immense value of our souls, by calling it the Price of
our Redemption. St. John incites us to love and gratitude towards this Blood, by holding it up as a token
of God's love and mercy, and as the precious burden
of the triumphant song of the elect. St. Paul has fairly
reddened the pages of his writings with references to
the Precious Blood, and thereby imbued us with a lively
hope and confidence in the mercy of God.

Among the Fathers, St. Chrysostom and St. Augustine show great zeal and devotion in speaking of the
Precious Blood. The former, thoroughly imbued with
veneration and all aflame with love towards the Sacred
Blood, represents it to us as a stream that irrigates
the entire earth, and by its fertility produces a rich
spiritual harvest. St. Ambrose calls the Blood of Christ
true gold of inestimable value. St. Bernard speaks of
the Precious Blood as a trumpet that calls to Heaven
for mercy. St. Thomas designates it as the key that
opens the heavenly treasures, just as it was the means
by which Heaven itself was opened to us.

St. Magdalen de Pazzi was all aglow with devotion
to the Precious Blood, and saw in this sea of mercy a
tide that leads all hearts to Jesus with sweet violence.
St. Gertrude saw the Precious Blood issue from the
wounds of the Saviour as from living springs and their
overflow fructifying the entire Church, even as the
rivers of Paradise irrigated that beautiful garden and
kept everything fresh, fragrant and blooming.

St. Francis de Sales said of St. Bonaventure, that
in his writings, he seemed to use no other ink that the
Blood of Christ. This expression, however, may be
applied with still more singular propriety to the writings of St. Catherine of Siena. She never began a letter without these words, "I write to you in the Precious
Blood." This name was never absent from her lips; the

one subject of her continual exhortations was that men should forget themselves, and keep the vessel of memory ever filled with the Blood of their Redeemer. "This Blood," she writes, "takes away all pain, and dispenses every joy; it deprives man of himself, and causes him to be absorbed in God." The power of this great saint over mankind was very wonderful. She seemed to be inebriated with divine love, which she drew from the fountain of the Precious Blood.

Those saints deserve special mention who were so highly favored as to bear the stigmata of Our Lord, and who, in their own blood oozing from hands and feet and side (like St. Francis of Assisi) could so beautifully—though with intense pain—contemplate the Precious Blood flowing from the Five Wounds of Jesus. This rare privilege of stigmatization indicates how much Our Saviour prizes the bloody wounds in His Sacred Body.

Let us remember also, that Our Lord has manifested himself to numerous saints (notably St. Margaret Mary Alacoque), all covered with His Blood; and that, in His Precious Blood, He still appears to saintly souls of our own day, offering us thereby fresh and continual proofs of His love for the "dyed garments from Bosra," and reminding us again and again of the great debt we owe to the Price of our Redemption.

In our own day, one of the most striking examples of Jesus appearing in His Blood is given to us by Father Germanus, the spiritual director of Gemma Galgani, who died in 1903. The servant of God had just finished the holy hour; she herself writes: "I found myself before Jesus Crucified. He was bleeding all over." She tells us of two salutary effects produced in her by the vision of Christ sweating blood. "The first," she said, "was to love Him, and love Him to sacrifice; the second was a great desire to suffer something for Him, seeing that

He had suffered so much for me." Two or three times, when ravished in the highest contemplation, she was heard to call her dear Lord "Spouse of Blood."

In the life of that most amiable little servant of God, Soeur Therese, who died in the odor of sanctity in the year 1897, we have another beautiful example of the efficacy of the Precious Blood to awaken in our hearts a burning love for God, and for souls redeemed in His Blood. In her autobiography we read as follows: "One Sunday, closing my book at the end of Mass, a picture of Our Lord on the Cross half slipped out, showing only one of His Divine hands, pierced and bleeding. I felt an indescribable thrill, such as I had never felt before. My heart was torn with grief to see that Precious Blood falling to the ground, and no one caring to treasure it as it fell; and I resolved to remain continually in spirit at the foot of the Cross, that I might receive the divine dew of salvation and pour it forth upon souls. From that day the cry of my dying Saviour—'I thirst,' sounded incessantly in my heart and kindled therein a burning zeal hitherto unknown to me.

"Was it not when I saw the Precious Blood flowing from the wounds of Jesus that the thirst for souls took possession of me? I seemed to hear Our Lord whispering to me, as He did to the Samaritan woman: 'Give me to drink!' It was indeed an exchange of love; upon souls I poured forth the Precious Blood of Jesus, and to Jesus I offered these souls, refreshed with the Dew of Calvary. In this way I thought to quench His thirst; but the more I gave Him to drink, so much more did the thirst of my own poor soul increase, and I accepted it as the most delightful recompense!"

On account of the prominence assigned by the Apostles themselves to the Blood of Christ as the instrument and price of our redemption and as the cause of the triumphs of the Blessed in Heaven, this devotion is pre-eminently called the "Devotion of the Elect." "Thou hast redeemed us, O Lord God, in thy blood out of every tribe and tongue and people and nation; and thou hast made us to become a kingdom unto our God." (*Apoc.* 5:9).

At the consecration of the chalice the priest uses these words: "For this is the chalice of my blood of the new and eternal testament, the mystery of faith which shall be shed for you and for many, to the remission of sins." While Christ indeed died for all men that all men without exception might be saved, the words, "For you and for many," imply that the fruits of His Precious Blood are not applied to all, because all men do not reach out for them, or co-operate with the proffered graces. In this sense we must also understand the prayer of Our Lord: "I pray for them whom thou hast given me, because they are thine." (*John* 17:9).

"This is the chalice of my blood which shall be shed for you." For me? My beloved Redeemer, I want to belong to those for whom Thou dost shed Thy Blood mystically every morning at Mass; for by this Blood I have become Thine own. "You are not your own, for you are bought with a great price. Glorify and bear God in your body." (*1 Cor.* 6:19-20). By venerating Thy Sacred Blood in a special manner, O Jesus, I want to become Thine own, in a particular manner, and to participate in a greater measure in the fruits of the Redemption.

Chapter 4

Growth and Development

JULY is the month dedicated to the Precious Blood, as it receives its consecration from the feast itself, which is celebrated throughout the entire Church on the first day of July. Pope Pius XI raised the feast to a higher rank.

It was the Lord Himself in the Old Testament who had called for the celebration of the feast of the Passover, in which the blood of lambs constituted a principal part, as a token and a pledge of God's mercy toward His chosen people. "And this day shall be for a memorial to you: and you shall keep it a feast to the Lord in your generations with an everlasting obser-vance." (*Ex.* 12:14).

Every Christian ought to observe the feast of the Pre-cious Blood in gratitude for his deliverance from the bondage of sin and Satan through the Blood and death of Christ on the Cross. "You are bought with a great price. Glorify and bear God in your body." (*1 Cor.* 6:20).

Devotion to the Precious Blood has sprung from a soil saturated, as it were, with the Blood of Christ. The history of Our Lord's Passion is written in His Blood; the pages of the Sacred Scriptures are reddened with it; the liturgical prayers of the Church are replete with invocations to the Blood of Reconciliation; and from our altars all over the world more than 300,000 chalices containing the Blood of the New Testament are daily uplifted for the salvation and sanctification of souls.

As the blood in the body circulates freely through its members, nourishing all its tissues and forming a medium upon which all the organs depend for their very life and functions, so, too, the Blood of Christ must naturally be traced in all the other devotions conveying supernatural life and grace, because the Blood of Christ underlies the whole plan of the Redemption and is the means of our sanctification in the sacraments.

The Eucharistic Blood of the Mass is the same redemptive Blood as that of Calvary and in this Blood we find the "riches of his grace" and the fruits of His Sacred Passion.

When we represent to ourselves the Blood of Jesus as pulsating in His arteries, we realize more vividly that it is not a phantom body, nor the body of Jesus as it was in the sepulcher, but the living Jesus as He appeared to His Apostles after the Resurrection, who is present in the Eucharist and whom we receive in Holy Communion.

"The life of the flesh is in the blood" and "it is the blood that gives testimony"—that is, bears witness to the sacred humanity of Christ. How often it has happened, that God has made use of blood upon the host or corporal, in order to convince some doubter of the Real Presence.

From the fact that the Church in her official liturgy has always practiced devotion to the Blood of Christ, it was but a natural consequence that a special devotion to this same Precious Blood should develop in the form of Confraternities and Congregations, into both active and contemplative Orders, which are already quite numerous.

There is also a Rosary or Chaplet of the Precious Blood, approved and highly indulgenced by the Church. The Archconfraternity of the Precious Blood is one of the richest and most highly privileged confraternities in the Church. Just as our Divine Saviour was prodigal in shedding His Precious Blood, so the Church is liberal in applying its merit to souls.

All spiritual writers agree that there is no more fruitful subject for meditation than the Passion of Our Crucified Saviour, and we know that every phase of His suffering is connected with the shedding of His Sacred Blood. What, then, is more fitting than that we should devote each of the seven days of the week to a meditation and oblation of the seven effusions of the Precious Blood.

A most consoling devotion to the Blood of Redemption and Atonement can be practiced at home every day of the week in the following manner:

On *Sunday* humbly ask Our Lord to offer to the Heavenly Father the Precious Blood of the Circumcision, together with the tears He shed during His earthly sojourn and the merits of His hidden and public life, for your sins of omission and your neglect in His service as well as your want of cooperation with His graces and inspirations.

On *Monday* pray Our Lord to offer to the Heavenly Father His Precious Blood which oozed out from every pore in the Garden of the Agony, together with His mental sufferings when fear, sadness, heaviness and disgust overwhelmed His soul, in expiation for all your sinful thoughts and desires against every virtue.

On *Tuesday* in a spirit of compunction beseech Our Lord to offer to His heavenly Father the Precious Blood flowing in streams from the widening wounds at the pillar of the scourging, together with the shame and the excruciating torments He endured, in expiation for your sins of impurity and especially as an atonement for the concupiscence of your eyes.

On *Wednesday* in a spirit of deep humility and contrition implore Our Lord to offer to His heavenly Father the Precious Blood shed in the crowning with thorns, together with the cruel mockery and the piercing pains He endured in the terrible torture of His Sacred Head, to atone for your pride, disobedience and anger.

On *Thursday* entreat Our Lord to make reparation to His Heavenly Father with the Blood flowing from the wound in His shoulder that stained the stones on His way to Calvary and marked the royal way of the cross, together with the tears and anguish of His Sorrowful Mother, for the sins you committed by giving scandal or by participation in the sins of others.

On *Friday* supplicate Our Lord to make atonement to His Heavenly Father for your sins of the tongue and all the sins you ever committed in word and deed, by offering the Precious Blood He so profusely shed in the Crucifixion amid unspeakable torments, together with the blasphemous taunting of His enemies and the burning thirst He endured on the Cross.

On *Saturday* with an humble and contrite heart plead with Our Lord to offer to His heavenly Father the Water and Blood that flowed from His Sacred Heart after His death, together with His generous forgiveness on the Cross, His utter dereliction and bitter death and the martyrdom of the Mater Dolorosa, in expiation for your sins against charity and the sins committed by your self-love and self-will.

These suggestions, carried out daily, one at a time—and it will take but a minute to do so, may be formulated in each one's own words. They will prove most profitable to the soul in life and in death. Some such devotion will also console Our Saviour, who complained by the mouth of the Prophet "what profit is there in my blood." (*Ps.* 29:10).

"Blessed are they that wash their robes in the blood of the lamb: that they may have a right to the tree of life, and may enter in by the gates into the city." (*Apoc.* 22:14).

Chapter 5

An Apostle of the
Precious Blood

THE illustrious Apostle of the Precious Blood, Blessed Gaspar del Bufalo, beatified by Pope Pius X, December 18, 1904, was born in Rome, on the feast of the Epiphany, January 6, 1786. He died in the Eternal City, December 28, 1837.

During the first and second years of his childhood, the little boy, of frail constitution, was twice threatened with serious ailments. But God, who disposes all things for the good of the elect, made use of the child's weakness to bestow upon him special favors. At this early age he was confirmed and thus received the fullness of the Divine Spirit. It is attested, that he never lost his baptismal innocence nor grieved the Holy Spirit by one serious sin. A severe attack of the measles affected his eyes to such an extent that it was feared he would remain blind for life. In her dire distress, his pious mother, Annunciata, had recourse to St. Francis Xavier, who seemed to have taken the little boy under his special protection, and obtained for him an almost instant cure. Later on, when Gaspar could realize the favor received from his benefactor, he chose the saint as his special patron and his while life was inspired by the deeds of the Apostle of India.

Before his twelfth year, Gaspar astonished his

125

parents, Antonio and Annunciata del Bufalo, by his deep and fervent piety. Every Thursday night, and also during the novenas to the Holy Ghost and to the Blessed Virgin, he slept on the bare floor. He even fasted, and wore a belt made of little pieces of tin, which he fastened, by a wire, so tightly around his tender body as to draw blood. When he told that it was unlawful to do this without the permission of his confessor, he at once ceased wearing it; but he did not neglect the practice of interior mortification, which is a surer test of sanctity.

He was called the little Aloysius. For three years he prepared himself constantly for Holy Communion. His ardent desire for the food of angels became a veritable fever. Often he would ask a companion returning from church: "What did Our Lord tell you today in Holy Communion?" Gaspar was eleven years old when he received his first Holy Communion in the chapel of St. Aloysius of the Collegium Romanum.

Even before he went to college, our little apostle was wont to gather around him the children of the street and to imbue them with a hatred of sin and with the love of God. As a student at the Collegium Romanum, he would invite his comrades to his house for spiritual conferences. Later on when he received minor orders he gave catechetical instructions to the poor people of the marketplace. In this manner, God prepared him for his missionary career.

Gaspar del Bufalo was ordained priest, July 31, 1808, and was at once made one of the canons of San Marco, Rome. Napoleon was just then in the zenith of his glory and, in 1809, sent Gen. Miollis to invade Rome and annex the Papal States. Excommunicated by Pius VII, Napoleon ordered the Pontiff to be taken into exile, along with the most notable of the clergy. When called upon to swear allegiance to the invaders, del Bufalo resolutely replied: "I cannot, I dare not, I will not." He was twenty-four years old when led into exile.

For nearly four years he had to suffer the greatest hardships in captivity. A severe sickness brought him almost to the point of death. He was crushed, so to speak, and tried by Our Lord in the furnace of tribulation. The seed of his future greatness and his glorious labors had been placed in the soil. Divine Wisdom now sent a saintly priest, Don Francesco Albertini, to water and nurture this seed with the Precious Blood of Jesus.

Albertini approached the dying Gaspar del Bufalo and told him that his earthly career was not yet over and, to prove his mission, communicated to him a prophecy which he had received from a saintly nun, Mary Agnes Schiavi, who had died the same year in the convent del Paolette, and to whose sanctity and supernatural gifts persons of the highest standing had testified. The prophecy was as follows: "You will find in a small church a young priest, who is full of zeal for the honor of God; when the enemy oppresses and torments you, then you shall enter into close friendship with him and become his spiritual adviser; a characteristic feature of his is a special veneration for St. Francis Xavier, and he is destined to become an apostolic missionary; he shall also establish a new congregation of Missionary Fathers under the invocation of the Precious Blood, for the reformation of the people and as a model to the secular clergy; he shall awaken the nations from their indifferentism and infidelity and arouse all to a love of the Crucified. He will be the trumpet of the Precious Blood and in evil times terrify sinners and sectarians."

At this time the Jesuit Order was restored by Pius VII. Del Bufalo applied to the General of the Jesuits for admission to the Order, and having been promptly admitted he returned home to make the necessary preparations. The next day, however, he received a summons to appear before Pius VII, who gave him orders to devote himself to missionary work. God had now spoken through the voice of His vicar upon earth, and Gaspar bowed immediately to His holy will, saying to the Pontiff, "I am at your service, Holy Father, I will do as you desire."

Gaspar del Bufalo laid the foundation of his new congregation, "The Missionary Fathers of the Precious Blood," August 15, 1815. It was never his intention to establish a regular religious order. His was to be a community of secular priests, banded together under a common rule by canon law, chiefly for the purpose of conducting diocesan missions and spiritual retreats. Their simple and ordinary mode of living, free from vows and any particular austerities, was to serve as a model to the secular clergy. The members were not only to practice devotion to the Precious Blood, but were to consider the spreading of this devotion an essential part of their mission.*

During the next twenty-three years, up to the time of his death, the Apostle of the Precious Blood, with his band of missionaries—many of whom died in the odor of sanctity—labored with astounding success, dividing his time between his missions and the task of organizing and developing his new society.

Our Lord once told Blessed Angela of Foligno that the word of the Gospel went with power to the soul only when it passed over the lips stained with His Precious Blood. Evidently Gaspar's singular eloquence received its impetus and its efficacy from the Blood of Jesus flowing from the Cross—that same Blood which, from its pulpit on Calvary, caused the rocks to split, the earth to quake, and the dead to rise. He was in

---

* *The Motherhouse of the Fathers C.PP.S. in the United States is at Carthagena, Ohio.*

truth "The Trumpet of the Precious Blood," as the saintly nun had prophesied.

The name, "Precious Blood," must have seemed very appropriate and beautiful to Cardinal Cristaldi, for on February 28, 1815, he wrote to Gaspar del Bufalo as follows: "The wish of the good Canon Albertini is also my wish, that the Congregation of the Missionaries be erected under the title of 'The Most Precious Blood of Jesus Christ'—that Blood which blots out sin, that Blood which saves souls, that Blood which gives power to the divine word, to the voice of the preachers and the missionaries, and which renders their labors in the vineyard of the Lord and for the salvation of souls so efficacious."

The last words of the saintly bishop, Francis Albertini, were: "Lord, for the sake of Thy Precious Blood let me hear these words which Thou didst speak to the penitent thief, 'This day thou shalt be with me in paradise.'"

He bound himself by a vow to spread this devotion, and everywhere on his missions he established the Archconfraternity of the Precious Blood.

Whenever he preached about the Precious Blood his face became flushed with enthusiasm; he was all fire and flame, and filled his audience with awe and wonder; he seemed to them like a supernatural being, and they would sob aloud, and drown his voice. It was at such times that he conquered the hearts of the most obstinate sinners. Even bishops followed him in admiration, and some laid aside their crosier and miter to join him in giving missions. He was truly a wonderful speaker. Ven. Bishop Strambi gave him the title of "Spiritual Earthquake." When the Bishop of Todi heard him conducting spiritual exercises for his clergy, he exclaimed publicly: "This is truly a man sent by God!"

"It is the Precious Blood," he wrote, "that destroys

sin, saves souls and lends power and fruitfulness to
the word of the missionary, *per sanguinem salvi facti
sumus.*" In his letter we find these words: "I feel the
devotion to Mary, the Blessed Virgin, increase in me,
but my devotion to the Divine Blood is something inexpressible. Oh, that I could spread this beautiful devotion with my own blood!" And again, "Would that I had
a thousand tongues to fill every heart with a love
towards the Most Precious Blood of Jesus, and nothing do I desire more than that souls might be imbued
with it."

When he saw the great armies of sin and irreligion,
with united forces, taking the field against the Crucified, he fairly burned with a desire to see the Blood
of his Redeemer honored and glorified. "Devotion to
the Precious Blood of Jesus Christ is the weapon of
our times," was one of his favorite sayings, quoting the
words of the Apocalypse, *"et ipsi vicerunt draconem per
sanguinem agni."* This roseate ensign of St. John: "And
they overcame him by the blood of the Lamb" (*Apoc.*
12:11), was made all the more glorious by the Apostle
of the Precious Blood in the nineteenth century. Under
this crimson banner all the elect in Heaven had fought
here on earth. By the Blood of the Lamb shed on the
Cross, by the Eucharistic Blood of the Lamb, slain, as
it were, in the Mass and received in Holy Communion,
they overcame the ancient enemy, Satan, and won their
crown in Heaven. The Blood of the Lamb on their banner fired them with love and zeal and soothed them
into patience and resignation to the Will of God.

So glorious a standard must have enemies. As a certain animal is infuriated by a red flag, so the devil is
enraged by the flaming ensign of the Precious Blood.
A true apostolate must be opposed from within and
without, but the enemies only help to render the banner all the more glorious. It was in the year 1830,

when his sufferings were at their height, that God consoled the holy missioner in a wonderful manner. While he was offering the Holy Sacrifice, Jesus showed him two golden chains that rose from the chalice, wound themselves around his body, and carried him up towards Heaven. His zeal was untiring. He often expressed a wish to die in the pulpit. In one of his letters to Cardinal Cristaldi we find these words: "If it is already so consoling to labor for God, what sweet repose must it be to rest in God."

Time and again the people were witness of the visible assistance and signal favors which God bestowed upon His apostolic servant. Once, during a sermon, a bright dove was seen to hover over his head. At the process of his beatification there was abundant testimony that he had possessed the gift of bilocation. During one mission a luminous cross was seen above his head; during another, a fiery ball; at Spello the entire congregation, together with the Bishop of Foligno, beheld three brilliant stars above him; at Gaeta he was seen to hover in the air while preaching, and he was understood by persons who did not know a word of Italian.

His deep humility was his constant safeguard against popular praise and applause which followed him everywhere on his missions. Often he would repeat the words of St. Paul: "When I was weak, then I am powerful." That this virtue was the result of conviction with him, is evinced by the fact, that at one time when he thought himself entirely alone, he was overheard saying: "I am doing nothing good." When the Fathers returned from their missions, he would kiss their hands, and repeatedly attempted to kiss their feet. Although founder and superior of the Community of the Precious Blood, he considered it his privilege to perform the most menial services in the household.

Much could be written of his missionary struggles, of his trials and tribulations; of his heroic virtues and austere penances; of the gift of prophecy which he possessed and which he manifested on numerous occasions; and of the many miracles wrought by him both before and after his glorious death, which he himself foretold; but for a more extensive account we must refer the reader to his 'Life' published by the Fathers of the Precious Blood, Carthagena, Ohio.

Blessed Gaspar del Bufalo died, it may be said, as a victim of his holy apostolate, in the fifty-second year of his age. He made a "libation, and offered of the blood of the grape. He poured out at the foot of the altar a divine odor to the most high Prince." (*Ecclus.* 50:16-17). Don Vincenzo Pallotti and Giovanni Merlini, who themselves died in the odor of sanctity and are awaiting the honors of the altar, assisted Gaspar del Bufalo in his last moments here on earth. To them he remarked, that he had now become as a little child. His first sermon as a young levite was on Divine Providence, and his last words were an expression of resignation to the holy will of God, "May the great will of God be done." "His face was radiant with joy and wore an expression of so sweet a peace, that I felt a desire for such a death struggle myself," says Pallotti. At the moment of Blessed Gaspar's departure from this life, Pallotti raised his hands and eyes towards Heaven and exclaimed: "O happy Soul!" He afterwards confided to Merlini that he saw the founder's soul in the form of a luminous star taking its flight to Heaven and our Lord Jesus Christ coming to meet His servant.

Seven days after his death, when his body was laid to rest, his tongue was still red and moist and his eyes as fresh as those of the living. His body showed no signs of decay and emitted a remarkably sweet odor. His remains are now preserved in the little church of

Santa Maria in Trevia, near the famous Fontana di Trevi, Rome. His feast is celebrated December 29.

If you have enjoyed this book, consider making your next selection from among the following . . .

2170 Blessed Marie Celine. *Poor Clares* 14.00
1890 Christian Perfection and Contemplation. *Garrigou-Lagrange.* 21.00
1882 Practical Commentary/Holy Scripture. *Bishop Knecht.* 40.00
0095 The Ways of Mental Prayer. *Dom Vitalis Lehodey* 16.50
1751 33 Doctors of the Church. *Fr. Rengers.* 33.00
1753 Pope Pius VII. *Prof. Robin Anderson* 16.50
1168 Life Everlasting. *Garrigou-Lagrange, O.P.* 16.50
1242 Mother of the Saviour/Our Interior Life. *Garrigou-Lagrange.* 16.50
1732 Three Ages/Interior Life. 2 Vols. *Garrigou-Lagrange, O.P.* .. 48.00
1261 Bl. Francisco Marto of Fatima. *Cirrincione,* comp. 2.50
1997 Bl. Jacinta Marto of Fatima. *Cirrincione* 3.00
1056 Facts About Luther. *Msgr. Patrick O'Hare* 18.50
1061 Little Catechism of the Curé of Ars. *St. John Vianney.* 8.00
1060 Curé of Ars—Patron Saint of Parish Priests. *Fr. B. O'Brien* .. 7.50
1052 Saint Teresa of Avila. *William Thomas Walsh* 24.00
1067 Isabella of Spain: The Last Crusader. *William Thomas Walsh* . 24.00
1053 Characters of the Inquisition. *William Thomas Walsh* 16.50
1054 Blood-Drenched Altars—Cath. Comm./Hist. Mexico. *Kelley* . 21.50
1057 Four Last Things—Death/Judgment/Hell/Heaven. *von Cochem* 9.00
1025 Confession of a Roman Catholic. *Paul Whitcomb* 2.50
1024 Catholic Church Has the Answer. *Paul Whitcomb* 2.50
1031 Sinner's Guide. *Ven. Louis of Granada* 15.00
1032 True Devotion to Mary. *St. Louis De Montfort* 9.00
1027 Life of St. Anthony Mary Claret. *Fanchón Royer* 16.50
1023 Autobiography of St. Anthony Mary Claret 13.00
1026 I Wait for You. *Sr. Josefa Menendez* 1.50
1034 Words of Love. *Menendez, Betrone, Mary of the Trinity* 8.00
0090 Little Lives of the Great Saints. *John O'Kane Murray* 20.00
1029 Prayer—The Key to Salvation. *Fr. Michael Müller.* 9.00
0080 Passion of Jesus and Its Hidden Meaning. *Fr. Groenings* 15.00
2121 Religious Vocation. *Butler* 12.50
0128 Canons and Decrees/Council of Trent. *Transl. Schroeder* ... 16.50
0748 Sermons of St. Alphonsus Liguori for Every Sunday 18.50
0078 Catechism of Modernism. *Fr. J. B. Lemius* 7.50
0094 Alexandrina—The Agony and the Glory. *Johnston* 7.00
0202 Life of Blessed Margaret of Castello. *Fr. William Bonniwell* . 9.00
1010 Catechism of Mental Prayer. *Simler* 3.00
0200 St. Francis of Paola. *Simi and Segreti* 9.00
0057 St. Martin de Porres. *Giuliana Cavallini.* 15.00
0056 Story of the Church. *Johnson, Hannan, Dominica* 22.50
0175 Hell Quizzes. *Radio Replies Press* 2.50
0161 Meditation Prayer on Mary Immaculate. *Padre Pio* 2.50
0063 Little Book of the Work of Infinite Love. *de la Touche* 3.50
1851 Textual Concordance of The Holy Scriptures. *Williams. pb.* . 35.00
1772 Which Bible Should You Read? *Thomas A. Nelson* 4.00
0104 The Way of Divine Love. *Sister Josefa Menendez* 21.00
2124 Gift of Oneself. *Schryvers* 14.00
0126 Mystical City of God—Abridged. *Ven. Mary of Agreda* 21.00

Prices subject to change.

1743 Visits to the Blessed Sacrament. *St. Alphonsus* 5.00
1280 Moments Divine—Before the Blessed Sacrament. *Reuter* ... 10.00
1222 Miraculous Images of Our Lady. *Cruz* 21.50
1223 Miraculous Images of Our Lord. *Cruz* 16.50
1963 Saints Who Raised the Dead. *Fr. Hebert* 18.50
1046 Love and Service of God, Infinite Love. *Mother Louise Marg.* 15.00
1045 Life and Work of Mother Louise Margaret. *Fr. O'Connell* ... 15.00
1042 Autobiography of St. Margaret Mary. 7.50
1043 Thoughts and Sayings of St. Margaret Mary 6.00
1035 Voice of the Saints. *Comp. by Francis Johnston* 8.00
1037 12 Steps to Holiness and Salvation. *St. Alphonsus* 9.00
1040 Rosary and the Crisis of Faith. *Cirrincione & Nelson* 2.00
1039 Sin and Its Consequences. *Cardinal Manning* 9.00
0200 St. Francis of Paola. *Simi and Segreti* 9.00
0150 Dialogue of St. Catherine of Siena. *Transl. Algar Thorold* ... 12.50
0752 Catholic Answer to Jehovah's Witnesses. *D'Angelo* 13.50
2172 Joy in Suffering. *Bishop Noser* 3.50
1019 Life of St. Aloysius Gonzaga. *Fr. Meschler* 13.00
1015 Love of Mary. *D. Roberto* 9.00
0323 Begone Satan. *Fr. Vogl* 4.00
0151 Prophets and Our Times. *Fr. R. G. Culleton* 15.00
0181 St. Therese, The Little Flower. *John Beevers* 7.50
0098 St. Joseph of Copertino. *Fr. Angelo Pastrovicchi* 8.00
0093 Mary, The Second Eve. *Cardinal Newman* 4.00
0361 Devotion to Infant Jesus of Prague. *Booklet* 1.50
1193 Reign of Christ the King in Public and Private Life. *Davies* . 2.00
0085 Wonder of Guadalupe. *Francis Johnston* 9.00
0312 Apologetics. *Msgr. Paul Glenn* 12.50
0191 Baltimore Catechism No. 1 .... 5.00
0192 Baltimore Catechism No. 2 .... 7.00
0147 Baltimore Catechism No. 3 .... 11.00
0119 Explanation of the Baltimore Catechism. *Fr. Kinkead* 18.00
0131 Bethlehem. *Fr. Faber* 20.00
0515 Bible History. *Schuster* 16.50
1244 Blessed Eucharist. *Fr. Mueller* 10.00
0307 Catholic Catechism. *Fr. Faerber* 9.00
0083 Devil. *Fr. Delaporte* 8.50
2173 St. Michael the Archangel. *Anonymous* 3.00
0148 Evidence of Satan in the Modern World. *Cristiani* 14.00
1339 Catholic Prayers (Small). *Traditional Sources* 4.00
2180 Catholic Prayers (Large). *Traditional Sources* 10.00
0338 Life of Anne Catherine Emmerich. 2 Vols. *Schmoeger.* 48.00
0107 Life of the Blessed Virgin Mary. *Emmerich* 18.00
0088 Manual of Practical Devotion to St. Joseph. *Patrignani* 17.50
1017 Prayerbook of Favorite Litanies. *Fr. Hebert* 12.50
0810 Preparation for Death. (Abridged). *St. Alphonsus* 12.00
1771 Purgatory. (From *All for Jesus*). *Fr. Faber* 6.00
1776 Bible History. *Johnson, Hannan, Dominica* 24.00
0155 Fundamentals of Catholic Dogma. *Ludwig Ott* 27.50
0108 Wife, Mother and Mystic. *Bessieres* 10.00
0163 Agony of Jesus. *Padre Pio* 3.00

Prices subject to change.

1721 Seven Capital Sins. *Benedictine Sisters* 3.00
1723 Confession—Its Fruitful Practice. *Benedictine Srs.* 3.00
1286 Sermons of the Curé of Ars. *Vianney* 15.00
1278 St. Antony of the Desert. *St. Athanasius* 7.00
0189 Is It a Saint's Name? *Fr. William Dunne* 3.00
0964 St. Pius V—His Life, Times, Miracles. *Anderson* 7.00
0156 Who Is Therese Neumann? *Fr. Charles Carty.* 3.50
0084 Martyrs of the Coliseum. *Fr. O'Reilly.* 21.00
1050 Way of the Cross. *St. Alphonsus Liguori* 1.50
1051 Way of the Cross. *Franciscan version* 1.50
1020 How Christ Said the First Mass. *Fr. Meagher* 21.00
0076 Too Busy for God? Think Again! *D'Angelo* 7.00
1014 St. Bernadette Soubirous. *Trochu* 21.00
1753 Pope Pius VII. *Anderson* 16.50
1525 Treatise on the Love of God. 1 Vol. *de Sales. Mackey, Trans.* 27.50
0173 Confession Quizzes. *Radio Replies Press* 2.50
1007 St. Philip Neri. *Fr. V. J. Matthews.* 7.50
1005 St. Louise de Marillac. *Sr. Vincent Regnault* 7.50
1002 Old World and America. *Rev. Philip Furlong* 21.00
0303 Prophecy for Today. *Edward Connor* 7.50
0062 Book of Infinite Love. *Mother de la Touche* 7.50
0118 Chats with Converts. *Fr. M. D. Forrest.* 13.50
0531 Church Teaches. *Church Documents* 18.00
0096 Conversation with Christ. *Peter T. Rohrbach* 12.50
0778 Purgatory and Heaven. *J. P. Arendzen* 6.00
1224 Liberalism Is a Sin. *Sarda y Salvany* 9.00
0077 Spiritual Legacy of Sr. Mary of the Trinity. *van den Broek* .. 13.00
0135 Creator and the Creature. *Fr. Frederick Faber* 17.50
0186 Radio Replies. 3 Vols. *Frs. Rumble and Carty* 48.00
0190 Convert's Catechism of Catholic Doctrine. *Fr. Geiermann* ... 5.00
0501 Incarnation, Birth, Infancy of Jesus Christ. *St. Alphonsus* ... 13.50
0055 Light and Peace. *Fr. R. P. Quadrupani* 8.00
0197 Dogmatic Canons & Decrees of Trent, Vat. I. *Documents* ... 11.00
0554 Evolution Hoax Exposed. *A. N. Field* 9.00
0091 Primitive Church. *Fr. D. I. Lanslots.* 12.50
0112 Priest, the Man of God. *St. Joseph Cafasso* 16.00
0134 Blessed Sacrament. *Fr. Frederick Faber* 20.00
0089 Christ Denied. *Fr. Paul Wickens* 3.50
0113 New Regulations on Indulgences. *Fr. Winfrid Herbst* 3.00
0127 A Tour of the Summa. *Msgr. Paul Glenn* 22.50
0168 Latin Grammar. *Scanlon and Scanlon* 18.00
0160 Brief Life of Christ. *Fr. Rumble* 3.50
0174 Marriage Quizzes. *Radio Replies Press* 2.50
0178 True Church Quizzes. *Radio Replies Press* 2.50
0106 Secret of the Rosary. *St. Louis De Montfort* 5.00
1001 Revelations of St. Bridget. *St. Bridget of Sweden* 4.50
0813 Magnificent Prayers. *St. Bridget of Sweden* 2.00
1006 Happiness of Heaven. *Fr. J. Boudreau* 10.00
1003 St. Catherine Labouré of the Miraculous Medal. *Dirvin* 16.50
0187 Glories of Mary. *St. Alphonsus Liguori* 21.00
1857 Three Conversions in the Spiritual Life. *Garrigou-Lagrange* . 7.00
Prices subject to change.

1880 Latin Mass Explained. *Moorman* 13.50
2180 Catholic Prayers. (Large Edition). *Traditional Sources* 10.00
2120 Little Nellie of Holy God. (children's). *Sr. M. Dominic* 8.00
1891 St. Margaret Clitherow—"The Pearl of York." *Monro* 6.00
1752 St. Vincent Ferrer. *Fr. Pradel, O.P.* 9.00
1749 The Life of Father De Smet. *Fr. Laveille, S.J.* 18.00
1747 Glories of Divine Grace. *Fr. Matthias Scheeben* 18.00
1593 Holy Eucharist—Our All. *Fr. Lukas Etlin* 3.00
1270 Hail Holy Queen (from *Glories of Mary*). *St. Alphonsus* 9.00
1265 Novena of Holy Communions. *Lovasik* 2.50
1219 Brief Catechism for Adults. *Cogan* 12.50
1215 Catholic Religion/for Child/Adult/Convert. *Burbach* 12.50
1047 Eucharistic Miracles. *Joan Carroll Cruz* 16.50
0199 The Incorruptibles. *Joan Carroll Cruz* 16.50
1738 Secular Saints: 250 Lay Men/Women/Children. PB. *Cruz.* . . 35.00
1058 St. Alphonsus Liguori. *Frs. Miller and Aubin* 18.00
1048 Self-Abandonment to Divine Providence. *Fr. de Caussade* . . 22.50
1049 Song of Songs—A Mystical Exposition. *Fr. Arintero* 21.50
0303 Prophecy for Today. *Edward Connor* 7.50
0504 Saint Michael and the Angels. *Approved Sources* 9.00
0390 Dolorous Passion of Our Lord. *Anne C. Emmerich* 18.00
0503 Modern Saints—Their Lives and Faces, Book I. *Ann Ball* . . . 21.00
1126 Modern Saints—Their Lives and Faces, Book II. *Ann Ball* . . 23.00
0203 Our Lady of Fatima's Peace Plan from Heaven. *Booklet* 1.50
0086 Divine Favors Granted to St. Joseph. *Père Binet* 7.50
0204 St. Joseph Cafasso—Priest of the Gallows. *St. John Bosco* . . 6.00
0807 Catechism of the Council of Trent. *McHugh/Callan* 27.50
0136 Foot of the Cross. *Fr. Faber.* 18.00
0185 Rosary in Action. *John Johnson* 12.00
0115 Padre Pio—The Stigmatist. *Fr. Charles Carty* 16.50
0162 Why Squander Illness? *Frs. Rumble & Carty* 4.00
0046 Fatima—The Great Sign. *Francis Johnston* 12.00
1012 Heliotropium—Conformity/Human Will to Divine. *Drexelius* 15.00
0750 Charity for the Suffering Souls. *Fr. John Nageleisen* 18.00
0159 Who Is Padre Pio? *Radio Replies Press* 3.00
0157 Stigmata and Modern Science. *Fr. Charles Carty* 2.50
0110 St. Anthony—The Wonder Worker of Padua. *Stoddard* 7.00
0132 Precious Blood. *Fr. Faber* 16.50
0164 Holy Shroud and Four Visions. *Fr. O'Connell* 3.50
0106 Secret of the Rosary. *St. Louis De Montfort* 5.00
0101 History of Antichrist. *Rev. P. Huchede* 4.00
1947 Where We Got the Bible. *Fr. Henry Graham* 8.00
0111 Hidden Treasure—Holy Mass. *St. Leonard* 7.50
0149 Imitation of the Sacred Heart of Jesus. *Fr. Arnoudt* 18.50
0075 Life and Glories of St. Joseph. *Edward Thompson* . . . .·. . 16.50
0184 Curé D'Ars. *Abbé Francis Trochu* 24.00
1013 Love, Peace and Joy. (St. Gertrude). *Prévot* 9.00

At your Bookdealer or direct from the Publisher.

Toll-Free 1-800-437-5876   Fax 815-226-7770
Tel. 815-226-7777   www.tanbooks.com

Prices subject to change.